My Pilot

A Story of War, Love, and ALS

Sarajane Giere

Imzadi Publishing, LLC

Copyright

Contents

To Bernie with love

Author's Note

This story is based on true events. However, it is a work of creative nonfiction and is my version of the truth. Certain names have been changed. In certain instances, dialogue has been reconstructed based on my memories and journals. Some might have different memories or interpretations of this story.

Prologue

Bernie and I as newlyweds, 1961.

Bernie set down his fortified fork—the handle thickened by tape for an easier grip—and settled back into his chair.

"Okay," he said, "shoot."

"Can you recall the first job you ever had?"

My pilot thought about it. Since he was in the early stages of ALS (amyotrophic lateral sclerosis) and willing to cooperate, I took every opportunity to ask about his childhood while we ate dinner. I'd told him I was writing a Giere family memoir.

"Let's see, my first job," Bernie began.

I opened the laptop next to my plate.

"When I was in elementary school, I shoveled snow in the narrow gateway between our house and the neighbors'. I had to carry each shovelful all the way to the front yard because there was no place to put the snow. I piled it up and it stayed there until it melted."

In fifty-one years of marriage, I hadn't heard that one. Bernie never complained about snow or any other circumstance out of his control, including his diagnosis. When the social worker asked what he thought about it, he'd said, "It is what it is."

Growing up in Chicago, near Lake Michigan, Bernie put up with harsh winters, knowing summer was on the horizon. He looked forward to kayaking with his dad in Diversey Harbor, a twenty-minute walk from the Giere house on Schubert Street.

I never tired of hearing about his early life, which was the opposite of mine. I was a suburban girl. The son of bourgeois German immigrants, Bernie had been brought up in a middle-class tradition of duty and discipline. His parents loved and coveted him as their oldest child, then their only child, after his younger brother died at age three. Bernie was seven.

I looked forward to dinnertime. My pilot across the table sometimes needed coaxing. Bernie's speech was slowly becoming more deliberate. At times he was just too tired to cooperate. Other times, I tactfully prodded him on, as if I were a journalist on a deadline. I suppose I did have a deadline. Most persons diagnosed with ALS, also known as Lou Gehrig's Disease, have three to five years left once they are diagnosed.

Bernie liked recalling his years at Lane Tech, a renowned high school of six thousand boys that produced its yearbook in its printing shop, repaired cars in its body shop, and offered classes in English and History for college-bound boys.

"What was it like playing football in Soldier Stadium for Lane Tech?" I asked, remembering that his mother told me he'd scored a touchdown during the city championship game. I hoped he'd recount the moment.

"When I was getting a routine physical before my senior year, the doctor found a heart murmur," Bernie said. "He told my parents I shouldn't play football. They were happy, but my coach wasn't. No football for me, my senior year."

There were summers working at a Wisconsin camp, where fourteen-year-old Bernie drove a truck, felled trees, shoveled gravel, and poured cement for tent floors.

"I was a counselor, too," he said. "I made foundations for three-hole outhouses. I dug the hole, made the forms and poured the foundation." This struck me as a heavy workload for a teenager, but it paid his way. I could tell he was proud of that. I was, too. It was a preview of a lifelong work ethic my pilot took for granted.

Our dinner sessions lengthened. Bernie reminisced about exercising at the local gym where the German immigrants' kids worked out. He delivered mail during holidays, installed garage doors, and worked with a labor gang. Then he landed at Coe College in Cedar Rapids, Iowa, where he met me and learned to fly through the United States Air Force ROTC program.

"We flew a little Tri Pacer propeller airplane at the Cedar Rapids airport. Only two out of five of us made it through the program," he said, grinning. "I was lucky."

Bernie and I married in September 1961, when my pilot had one semester left at Coe. I worked at the telephone company and rode the bus home when it was thirty below zero. For newlyweds like us, the temperature was only mildly disconcerting. We were safe and warm in our cozy attic apartment.

I burst with pride at Bernie's commissioning, a ceremony held by the ROTC department upon his graduation in January 1962. The captain in charge asked if I would make my husband an official second lieutenant by pinning a gold bar on his uniform.

"Of course," I replied, reining in my enthusiasm to befit the serious occasion. I saved the hurrahs until we returned home. There were plenty!

A few months later we left for a year at Webb Air Force Base in Texas where Bernie would learn to fly jet aircraft and I would learn to become an air force wife. We were so much in love that we never questioned what the future would bring. We knew Bernie would have a steady paycheck during his five-year commitment to Uncle Sam. We knew there would be travel, but we didn't know what kind or where it would take us.

In the winter of 1962, our life together lay ahead like a red carpet. Challenges were waiting to test us.

PART 1

"Absence is to love, what wind is to fire; it extinguishes the small; it enkindles the great."

— Roger de Rabutin

Chapter 1

BIG GAME HUNTER

Living in Big Spring would surprise me. In the summer of 1962, the Texas town welcomed me with those confounded dust devils—mini tornadoes that grabbed up the sand and flung it through our windows. Bernie, the student pilot, didn't mind, but I did. He was busy at nearby Webb Air Force Base, trying out the T-37 jet trainer. I was looking for a job.

The base was alive with testosterone—wild costume parties, late-night sessions at the Officers Club bar, and water polo contests. Comprised mostly of recent college graduates, the squadron members and their wives got together often, staging parties for every occasion. Bernie earned his wings that year, flying the T-37 and T-38.

I adjusted well to being an air force wife. My mother had taught me *not* to be shy when meeting strangers or, as she called it in her business world, "working a room." I wanted to feel comfortable among the wives and establish my place among them, even if just for a year.

Many couples played bridge. Those who didn't know how eventually learned. Some gatherings lasted into the wee hours. When we hosted the game the couple next door, who had a baby, called our house. I answered and left the phone off the hook. Then they came over and we set the receiver near the card table. When we heard the baby cry, the couple went home.

I knew we were at the beginning of Bernie's five-year military career, so I had no qualms about missing the morning and afternoon wives' coffees while I was at the office. We'd be moving on to a longer assignment and then I'd have time to be a housewife. In Big Spring I preferred to work and considered myself lucky to land a position in a small, air-conditioned office. I wanted to polish my service representative skills and see what small-town Texans were like.

Mr. Travis Tucker, the new manager at Southwestern Bell Telephone Company, recently arrived from his hometown of Dallas—the big city five hundred miles to the east where he'd hoped to be assigned. Jean, who supervised the five women in the office, welcomed me.

"Mr. Tucker was impressed with your experience and your recommendations," she said. "He hired you on the spot! Unheard of, girl. Good for you."

My new friend walked me through everything from office procedures to the town's history. She also told me what happened when the tornado siren goes off.

"The pilots will take the planes to safety in New Mexico," she said, "and you'll be on your own." *Really?*

I soon discovered I was the only pilot's wife who had a job. It gave me notoriety and us an extra paycheck.

Bernie and I read each evening after dinner. He had his latest James Michener novel, and I delved into my new manual by author Nancy Shea, *The Air Force Wife: What the Wives of Officers Ought to Know about the Customs of the Service and the Management of an Air Force Household.*

"Listen to this, Bernie: 'Homemaking is a full-time job and a wife should not work unless there is a real need for the money

18

she earns. If you're working simply to buy a car or piano, it's not a worthwhile reason.'" *How condescending! My mother always worked. Why shouldn't I?*

Bernie put his book down.

"Honey, I'm proud you're working," he said. "She's not talking about you."

"There's more: 'If you do work, always remember that your husband and your home come first, and it is not correct to expect your husband to accept a slapdash sort of homemaking." *Slapdash? Me?*

"No, honey. You're a little absentminded at times, but not slapdash."

Bernie was probably thinking of the time I shortened his cotton, summer uniform pants before I washed them in hot water. I didn't know that hot water shrank cotton. They looked okay to me as I hung them on pants stretchers on my backyard clothesline, just like his mother used to do. The next morning as I made breakfast, Bernie's lament reached me from the bedroom.

"What the hell? High-waters!"

I learned at that moment that cotton shrank and there was no learning curve for the military wife: we had to do things right the first time.

The colonel welcomed us wives gathered in the base lecture hall. He smiled while he admonished us to be good. He told us if we so much as bounced a check, our husband's squadron leader would find out.

"Everything you do, good or bad, reflects on your husband's career," he said. "And ladies, your husbands can't perform successfully with domestic worries on their minds."

I remembered these warnings when I had to discontinue telephone service to a pilot because his wife made daily long-distance calls to her mother in Europe. They could not pay the bill. Tra-

19

vis helped me and worked things out with the base commander, though. So many couples, so many problems. I was earning a psychology degree, but I didn't know it at the time.

Before he dismissed us, the colonel warned: "Ladies, it's been a pleasure. And let me say this: if you aren't pregnant now, most of you will be by the time you leave here." The audience tittered. I didn't. *Not me.* Who was he to tell me when I would conceive?

When I told Jean about the colonel, she couldn't believe it, either.

"How embarrassing," I said. "I feel like a statistic."

"You wait and see, Sarajane. You've got a year to go."

Travis, still high from his weekend adventures, looked happy as he strode into the office on Mondays. We reps sat at our desks like schoolgirls in homeroom waiting for the teacher.

"How y'all this mornin'?" Travis asked, as he walked past our desks to the coffeepot, nodding to each of us. A short man with a big strut, he had a plume of thick, black hair combed into a pompadour. He propped his gun case against the file cabinet and poured coffee into his hand-painted, ceramic mug shaped like a deer's head.

Jean winked at me from across her desk.

"I'm just fine, Mr. Tucker." She lifted her eyebrows and grinned. "How was your weekend?"

Travis set his mug near the edge of my desk, smoothed back his shiny mane, rubbed his hands together, and smiled like a Cheshire Cat.

"Well, ladies, I'd say a jackrabbit shoot is one of the greatest cures for the summertime blues. No, I take that back. I'll say it *is* the greatest cure, especially out here in West Texas."

I piped in.

"And why is that, Mr. Tucker?"

Travis paused, thought for a minute, looked down at his handcrafted cowboy boots, and then back at me and Jean. His boots matched the tan in his plaid, polyester sport coat.

"You see, ladies, it's the thrill of the game, that's what it is. It takes you away from your everyday routine." From my desk I could see the ornate, polished oak in his office. His gun rack, against the wall, had one empty slot. There was a gold trophy on his file cabinet, next to a framed photo of a big game hunter in camouflage.

"I've never even seen a jackrabbit," I continued, "but then, I'm a city girl from Saint Louis, Mr. Tucker, and I don't know much about hunting."

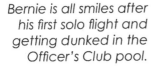

Bernie is all smiles after his first solo flight and getting dunked in the Officer's Club pool.

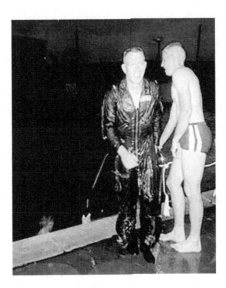

Jean cupped her hand over her mouth and turned away. When Travis started to tell us about his new Ruger Takedown rifle, a customer mercifully walked in. The Boss whispered loudly, "Tell y'all later," toted his rifle, and disappeared into his office.

I remember that day, especially the lunch afterwards. We girls trotted over to the fourteen-story Settles Hotel—the highest building in town. We sat at the U-shaped café counter, facing all the regulars opposite us. Those good ol' boys wanted to know what we thought of our boss, the new dude from Dallas.

"He sure can shoot," one of them said. We giggled but remained polite and said we were just getting to know Mr. Tucker.

On our way home from work later, Jean told me that Travis and the good ol' boys wait until dark, then circle their pickups around, headlights glaring, like a wagon train fending off the Indians. Only this time, the victims inside the circle can't shoot back. Startled by the lights, those poor jackrabbits, some as big as German shepherds, hop and flop around like crazy, trying to find their way out.

"How disgusting! How sad!" I said. "Doesn't sound as if they have a chance."

Jean looked at me with a combination of wry humor and compassion.

"Not if Travis can help it."

"Well, he's no Davy Crockett, that's for sure," I said, as we reached my place. "See you tomorrow."

Jean waved, and as she pulled away, she called out.

"Sara, now that you've been broken in, you can call him Barney Fife," she said. "We all do."

In spite of our disrespectful humor, Travis proved to be an effective manager though none of us admitted it at first. He backed me up when I was confronted by a disgruntled customer and taught me sales strategies. He rewarded me every time I met my quota for the month with another telephone charm for my Southwestern Bell bracelet. By the time I left a year later, it jingled. Of the six bosses I've had in my life, Travis is the only one I remember in Technicolor.

Meanwhile, Bernie earned his wings that year. He was dunked—with flight suit on—in the Officer's Club pool after he soloed in the T-37. The party commenced, with many more to follow as each pilot gained his wings.

We were off to a new assignment in Tampa after our Texas year, looking forward to the birth of our first child in two months. We took happy memories of Big Spring with us, and the realization that it was the people, not the place, that counted.

Expectant parents,
Bernie's Pilot graduation day, Big Spring, TX.

Chapter 2

SECRETS IN THE DESERT

In the fall of 1963 we left Texas and headed for MacDill Air Force Base in Florida. Our thoughts were filled with our first child's birth and Bernard's new squadron. He got a plum assignment flying the newest jet plane—the two-seat, twin-engine, all-weather supersonic F-4 Phantom II. It flew at Mach 2, twice the speed of sound, and carried a payload of up to sixteen thousand pounds of bombs, rockets, missiles, and guns. Each aircraft had 54,197 feet of wiring and was held together by 643,000 fasteners.

But Bernard would be gone a lot at jump school in Georgia and on cross-country trips for war games. He'd be in Okinawa for three months and in Vietnam for a year. I had to adapt, though his adventures took him to places he shouldn't have been where he saw things he shouldn't have seen. I didn't complain: homecomings were honeymoons.

Those Tampa years were full of surprises and a test of my faith and fortitude. I wanted to know everything Bernie did on his cross-country trips, but he could only tell me so much. Many experiences were for pilots' ears only.

One incident happened on a TDY (temporary duty yonder) to Nellis Air Force Base near Las Vegas. Bernard was flying with his good friend Wally. They executed low-level penetration test runs to see how fast the airplanes could go on a flat course. After each pass the jet blast and shock waves blew the concrete-filled, bright orange barrels that marked each run all over the place. Airmen in a jeep had to retrieve and reset them. On that flat course, the airplane averaged Mach 1.3 (nearly 1,000 mph) at twenty-eight feet above the ground. The pilots established performance records that would prove valuable in Vietnam.

F-4's under overcast skies.

On one such pass Wally and Bernie spotted a weird, black-shaped airplane flying nearby. They had some extra fuel, so they flew over to see if it wanted to play. It didn't, but by the time they realized it, they'd ventured into the famous Lockheed test-proving grounds known as the "Skunkworks." When they returned to Nellis they were met by security people, who debriefed them. Bernie and Wally described the mysterious black plane they saw and were immediately admonished.

"If you tell anyone about this," they were told, "we'll burn your eyes out."

They'd seen an experimental SR-71, known as the Black-bird—a top-secret, long-range, high-speed stealth, aerial recon-naissance warplane.

When Bernie told me this years later, I took him at his word but had to laugh at the burn business. I'd always been curious to see the actual Blackbird. In 1997, I finally did. We were standing by the flight line at a Nellis air show with Wally and his wife, Arlys. Hundreds of onlookers surrounded us as desert heat wafted upward from the pavement and waves of vintage aircraft droned overhead.

Suddenly I saw it—a triangle, flat, black and wide, flying through the air as silently as a hawk sailing for the kill. No noise or afterburners, just eerie silence. I grabbed Bernie's arm.

"Is that it?"

"Yep. That's the SR-71, honey. The secret spy airplane. The Blackbird."

"I always thought it was a little bit much. Burn your eyes out?"

"I would have lost my job, perhaps my life, if I'd told anyone."

Bernie and Wally smiled as they remembered their thirty-three-year-old caper.

Bernie had embraced the move from Texas to Tampa with happy anticipation, but I wasn't sure about Florida. I imagined it as another hot spot with big, crawling bugs and spiders, devoid of autumn colors and temperatures. But Bernie reminded me how many friends we'd made in Texas.

"Didn't you get a kick out of working with those good ol' boys down there?" he asked.

I had to admit he was right. I loved it. I behaved as my *Air Force Wife* manual advised: "Adjust to your environment. Make the best of whatever comes without assuming a martyr-like at-titude. It is always unwise complaining about places and bases you've never seen."

I saw how proud Bernie was to be a member of the 555th Fighter Squadron, nicknamed the Triple Nickel, at MacDill. His sense of accomplishment showed in the way he carried himself, the pep in his step, and his can-do attitude.

"I'm one of the lucky ones," Bernard said in his self-effacing way. He talked as if this new plane were his baby taking its first giant steps. "The F-4 Phantom set the world speed record of 1,604 mph. They're so many of them now, they're still rolling off the assembly line at McDonnell Aircraft in Saint Louis."

I heard a lot about those afterburners.

"Just you wait," Bernard said. "I'll take you to the flight line so you get an earful."

The Triple Nickel squadron, deactivated after World War II, was reemerging at MacDill, which was filled with pilots from other squadrons. All were under the command of the 12th Fighter Wing. The base was a beehive.

The day we arrived in Tampa, September 2, 1963, was a record breaker: it was the hottest day of the year, the telephone company was on strike, base housing quarters were filled up, I was seven months pregnant, and it was our second wedding anniversary. What a welcome!

We stayed at a motel outside the base gates across from a diner that advertised, in yellow letters, "Complete Breakfast, 35 cents—two eggs, bacon, grits, toast and coffee." We learned the next morning the owner had rolled prices back to 1925, the year of his birth. We began each day there over bacon and eggs, thinking it might be a harbinger for good luck.

While Bernie became adjusted to his new squadron, I called realtors from the telephone booth outside the motel—the only working phone around. The sun's rays turned the booth into a sauna as I thumbed through the yellow pages for brokers. One sympathetic soul showed me a rental house nearby, six blocks from MacDill.

"I'll take it," I said, admiring its wide, screened-in porch. It seemed to compensate for the dinky wall-heater and antiquated air-cooling system.

MacDill jutted out into Tampa Bay. The palatial generals' homes faced the water. The rest of base-housing, modestly folded in among other buildings, was vintage World War II. The airplane hangars impressed me. They were the same ones that appeared in the 1956 movie, *Strategic Air Command*. In my mind's eye I saw Jimmy Stewart strolling those mammoth hangar-caves, admiring impressive B-47s, the precursors of the B-52 Bomber.

June Allyson, Jimmy's movie wife, hadn't bargained on being an air force wife. I had. She groused. I tried not to. I didn't want to complicate matters. Why give my pilot anything else to worry about?

My next concern was the birth of our baby in November at the impressive multistory base hospital. I waltzed in to sign up but was told there was absolutely no room in maternity. *Are they serious?*

"You will have to deliver on the economy," the captain said. I sat down.

"What's that?"

"It's when we give you a chit for twenty-five dollars and you choose your own doctor and hospital in Tampa—Saint Joseph's Hospital or Tampa General. Take your pick."

"But my husband and I just arrived here," I peeped. "We haven't a clue when it comes to Tampa doctors."

"I see." He paged through papers on his desk. "Second Lieutenant Bernard Giere with the Triple Nickel?"

"Yes", I answered, sitting up a little straighter, hands in my lap.

"I'm sorry," he stated. "We have no room."

I asked if he could recommend any doctors. He said that was not allowed.

When Bernie heard my disappointment, he reassured me.

"Don't worry honey, I'll take care of it."

The next day he went to the hospital to set things right. He called.

"It's a no go, hon," he said. "If you had begun your pregnancy here, it would be different. We'll have to get some recommendations."

I sped back to the maternity wing and found a sympathetic-looking secretary. Her desk was rife with manila folders but in the midst of the mess were fresh flowers in a mason jar. I introduced myself and chatted about how much I liked being in Tampa. I repeated what I'd heard the day before and how I felt about it, raising my voice as I went along and throwing up my hands.

She sighed as if none of this was new.

"That's right, Mrs. Giere," she quipped. "We are not allowed to recommend any Tampa doctors. I'm sorry. Military regulations, you know."

Two nurses across the hall turned and glanced at me. I lowered my voice. I had an idea. I inched my way over and grabbed the yellow pages from the cabinet behind her desk. I flipped it open to "Obstetricians," plopped it down in front of her and said, "Point."

She did. The name under her pointer finger was Dr. Stephens, a lovely man who delivered our daughter at Tampa's Saint Joseph's Hospital. I liked St. Joe's so much, I chose it for our son's birth two years later.

Our house on Oklahoma Avenue was comfortable. Squadron get-togethers at the Officer's Club kept us entertained, and I enjoyed the comradery among the wives. Ed, our next-door neighbor and a native Floridian, invited us to the bay to go treasure hunting and wade in the turbulent waves from Hurricane Ginny, dallying off shore.

"We'll find some goodies," Ed promised. He pointed out the awkward brown pelicans swooping low over us. "Believe it or not," he said, "their beaks can hold more than their bellies."

I dug up a huge conch shell with my toes and a brown cockle bigger than my hand. Back on the beach, Bernie displayed his treasure—a shark's tooth.

"Lucky you," Ed said. "That's what's left of a shark who probably inhabited these waters millions of years ago."

Ahead of us was Tampa General Hospital on Davis Island, just across a flimsy bridge to mainland Tampa. I wondered how often the bridge flooded and was instantly gratified I'd chosen Saint Joseph's Hospital.

Gretel, or Oma, as she'd be called, flew down to Tampa to be with us for the month. Though it was her first flight, she wasn't hesitant. This was her first grandchild, and if Bernard said she had nothing to fear, it must be true.

Lisa was born in the early morning of November 6, 1963. Bernard drove me to the hospital the night before while his mother paced our house and planned her special meal to celebrate her first grandchild's arrival. Lt. Giere strolled the hospital waiting room all night, tinkering with and tamping down his new pipe. By the next morning, the pipe was worn out. So was my pilot. (In those days, men weren't allowed in the labor or delivery rooms.)

Bernie called his mother at 7:30 a.m. and then Rudolf, the new Opa, in Chicago. I was above it all, lying on a cloud, cuddling my precious little Lisa.

"I'm soaking meat for sauerbraten," Gretel told me at the hospital. It would take about five days to soak. By that time, Rudolf would have arrived in Tampa. I thought of my little kitchen and how it was going through another kind of labor, the painless kind: Oma bustling, arranging pots and pans, realigning my cooking tools, cleaning out the refrigerator, preparing for the homecoming.

Bernard and I were enthralled with ourselves for creating such a dainty, little masterpiece. Parenting seemed a natural manifestation of our love.

Oma gave good advice on baby tending. I was content to stay out of her kitchen and nurse my baby.

"Nursing mothers must drink beer," Oma said, "or else you'll be dehydrated!" She cleaned and cleaned some more, knitted at night, and kept us all well fed.

Rudolf had driven down from Chicago with their miniature dachshund, Schnapps. Opa was pleased by Oma's sauerbraten, potato dumplings, and Rhine wine, and Schnapps was happy with all the attention.

Bernard enjoyed showing his parents Tampa. A base tour was the highlight. Yes, the afterburners of the F-4's two 17,000-pound thrust G.E. jet engines would blow anyone away if they weren't careful. He told his parents to hold their ears. And Rudolf learned the guard at the base gate was saluting the lieutenant sticker on the car as they entered, and not waving hello to the lieutenant's father.

We learned President Kennedy was coming to Tampa the following week, on Monday, November 18, and would take a motorcade from the airport to MacDill. We weren't Kennedy fans so we decided to stay home.

"Too much hubbub," Oma said.

JFK would make three speeches that morning and two more in Miami that afternoon. The *Tampa Tribune* wrote he was "closeted" in a secret session at MacDill with General Paul Adams, commanding officer of the base's Strike Command, a rapid deployment force to trouble spots such as Cuba. The newspaper also mentioned that security had been heightened because authorities had been warned of a possible assassination attempt. I thought this news rather shocking but heard no more about it.

Bernard told me the pilots and their planes were organized into squadrons. Each squadron had twenty-five planes and their pilots. His squadron, the 555th, was part of MacDill's Twelfth Fighter Wing. There could be as many as four squadrons to a wing. At MacDill these squadron units were created during the Cuban Missile Crisis of 1962 when pilots were called up to active duty from the air force reserve units. Bernie discovered there were still contingency plans in the pilots' briefing room, such as strip maps of Cuba highlighting targets.

Planes parked in Naha, Okinawa.

When Lisa was two weeks old, we took her on her first outing to Busch Gardens, Tampa's newest tourist park. After an hour strolling the gardens, Oma said she'd manage the baby buggy and stay with Lisa in the courtyard while Bernard and I took Rudy through the five-story brewery. We rode the outside escalator, called Stairway to the Stars, to the top of the brewery, where the tour began. I spotted the tourists below and saw Gretel talking to a man and woman. Our group passed through the brewery to see how beer was made and drank our cups of beer samples. I looked out as we took the glass elevator down and saw people going to and from the parking lot. Oma was talking to more people.

"Something's going on," Bernie mused. We hurried to reach Gretel when we touched the ground.

"This man heard on his car radio that the president and vice president have been shot," Gretel said.

"Where was he?" Bernie asked.

"In Dallas," the man said. Gretel's voice came in a whisper and her eyes blinked wide as she took in all the activity around us. People hurried to their cars. They were going home. We stood there in disbelief. Surely this was a mistake. Wasn't the President just here? We, too, headed for our car and home where we watched history unfold through our Motorola television set in the living room.

"We'll never forget this sad day," Rudy said. It had been ninety-eight years since Lincoln was murdered.

At a loss for words, I hugged Lisa and walked back and forth from TV to kitchen. The weekend flashed by. Walter Cronkite and Dan Rather held camp in our living room. They were our TV detectives in this ongoing, tragic murder mystery. Where did this Lee Harvey Oswald come from, anyway? There was Jackie under a black veil with her two sweet children. How they tugged at my heart. I thought of how vulnerable we all are. If someone as guarded as our president could fall from an assassin's bullet, how safe could we be?

Bernard went back to work Monday. The rest of us went on with our chores and took care of Lisa. Schnapps, a champion lap sitter, lifted our spirits.

Our television news became addictive. The tragedy brought me closer to my in-laws. Emotional strangers no more, we assuaged our grief and mourned in one tight unit with hugs, tears, and miles of speculations. I no longer saw them as German Americans but as

Americans like me. The veil came down. They had gone through tragic losses, losing their parents during WWII and their three-year old son, Carlie, in 1943.

Lisa, asleep in her little crib on wheels, was parked next to me as police transported Lee Harvey Oswald. I watched Jack Ruby shoot Oswald as I knitted a shell sweater Oma had designed for me. My hands froze in place. Another tragedy, worse than any of Shakespeare's, was unfolding. *This can't be happening.* We asked each other, "When will this all end?"

Rudy and Gretel took Schnapps back to Chicago because Opa had to return to work, but our house didn't stay empty for long. The news of the day was of Lyndon Johnson and the new administration, including snippets of activities occurring in Vietnam. I was preparing for company. My parents, Patty and John, were coming from Saint Louis to spend Christmas with us.

Mother brought her Siamese cat, Mario. I had agreed to keep him when she called the week before. "The poor guy doesn't like apartment living," my mother had said, "and I don't know what to do with him."

"Sure, Mother. We have a roomy house with a screened-in porch, and our neighbor Ed has a Siamese, too." Bernie agreed. How could we have been that gullible?

The cat was named after the lead character in the opera *Tosca*, Mario the artist, who was madly in love with the singer, Tosca. My Mario lived up to his namesake's reputation. He prowled for females and fought with males, especially our neighbor Ed's Siamese cat, Snoopy, a brawler with half an ear and one eye. Mario sprayed urine on my living room drapes, which I later found out was typical of an "intact" male.

"Perhaps a trip to the vet would be in order," Mother said. "I wanted to have it done in Saint Louis, but the vet said Mario was too old."

My parents loved their son-in-law's Tampa tours. Lisa was a great little traveler so we drove to Sarasota and other spots along the coast, too. I was thrilled to have my folks with us for Lisa's first Christmas, and I lived for each moment, knowing they'd be gone soon and it wouldn't be long before Bernard would be, too. He'd be staying three weeks at Fort Benning, Georgia to earn his parachute wings.

After my parents left and while Bernie was shaping up for jump school, my "Holy shit, I've had it" moment came upon me. I was bathing Lisa in the bathroom sink when I heard a low hiss rise to a crescendo and become a piercing wail. The cacophony sounded as if Mario and Snoopy were tearing each other apart. I peeked outside to see, and they seemed to be doing just that. *Yikes!*

I rolled Lisa in a towel, laid her in her crib, and ran outside with a broom, yelling at the little beasts. They kept at it, so I turned on the hose and shot jets of water between them until the weary warriors finally peeled away. I called Bernard. The next day he took Mario to the base veterinarian to be patched up and neutered.

The vet said it would have been healthier if Mario were neutered as a kitten, but he fixed him anyway. From then on, our docile cat behaved himself.

My pilot relished the rigorous training before and during jump school at Fort Benning. It was the ultimate test of fitness, nerves, and determination. Fat men needn't apply. Bernard went with another Triple Nickel pilot. They ran together to get in shape. At Fort Benning trainees ran everywhere. Why walk when you can run?

"That's the army way," Bernie said.

Bernie's running partner consumed nothing but Diet Coke for two weeks. He had to lose ten pounds. They made it through. Bernie remembered their trial-by-army experiences forty-eight years later at our dining room table:

We did a lot of push-ups and sit-ups. Sergeants—big muscular guys who ordered you around—were our instructors. We practiced parachute landing falls—when you jump off a four-foot embankment and do a parachute landing roll. You learn to cushion your fall when you hit the ground.

We practiced how to exit the airplane from a thirty-four-foot tower. You were hooked to a cable and exited through a mock door, grabbed your reserve chute, and rolled down the cable. There was a young army recruit who stopped in the door, his knees shaking so badly that he wouldn't move. The instructor kicked him in the butt and said, "Get off my ******* tower." I was next and smartly stepped out the door. I wasn't nervous.

Life on the ground wasn't much easier:

One day we were doing calisthenics and an F-4—from a training area nearby—did low rolls over us and left. Everyone stopped to watch it, the newest jetfighter in use. The instructor said to me, "Lieutenant, what kind of an airplane was that?"

I said, "That was an F-4C, sergeant."

"That airplane just interrupted my class. Do you fly that airplane, lieutenant?"

Proud as heck, I said, "Yes, sergeant."

"Then," he said, "come up here and give me fifty pushups."

Upon his return Bernie was so lean and fit, he resembled himself at age fifteen. He was pure muscle and his uniform pants were a 31-inch waist. The wings on his uniform had a parachute on top. We turned our attention to shopping for our first house. That summer of 1964 we bought a three-bedroom ranch-style house near the base while the squadron prepared for its first big deployment, a ninety-day TDY in Okinawa. I suppose they knew war was coming but I couldn't think about that. I was making curtains for our cozy home.

On December 8, 1964 Bernie and the 555th flew the F-4C Phantom II fighter interceptors to Okinawa for a three-month stay. It would be the first time the multi-purpose planes with nuclear capabilities had been sent to land bases in the Orient. The eighteen planes of the 555th would be stationed at Naha on a ninety-day rotational basis with other units in the US.

Bernard explained his role as a pilot in the F-4:

I was a back seater with Wally as the pilot. I was called either a PSO (pilot systems operator) or GIB (guy in the back seat). I ran the radar and the inertial navigation system. We sat air defense alert for twenty-four hours at a time, but we never scrambled for real, only on an exercise when the F-105s or T-Birds (T-33s) came down from Japan to test the radar operators and us. The F-102 interceptors were there, but they were tired old airplanes so we replaced them.

In Okinawa Bernie lived in a barracks called the BOQ (bachelor officers' quarters), where local maids did all the men's laundry. He'd written me that the maids laughed when he told them the child in the framed photo on his dresser was our one-year-old daughter, Lisa, in a sailor-suit dress. They'd thought she was a boy.

"You should have seen them giggle when I told them they were wrong," he wrote. "That little sailor was our Lisa."

Years later, in 2017, I read that storage of the Agent Orange herbicide in Okinawa was controversial, as described in Amy Chavez's "Growing Evidence of Agent Orange in Japan" (*Huffington Post*). Our government denied it despite the airmen who said they had used it as a weed killer at some bases there. Other servicemen saw the distinctive cans of herbicide being stock-piled at various locations. Bernie might have been exposed when he escorted the C-123s, which defoliated areas in South Vietnam in 1965 and 1966. In 2019 I spoke with Bernie's Cam Ranh Bay roommate, Danny, who told me their F-4s flew under the spray planes (C-123s) through the clouds of Agent Orange when they strafed the Viet Cong machine nests below. The F-4 pilots flew into these conditions with their masks on in the "normal" mode, breathing unfiltered air.

ALS is not linked to Agent Orange exposure. Nevertheless, the VA presumes that it is related to service in diagnosed veterans who served at least ninety continuous days. The VA calls ALS and other diseases such as Parkinson's "presumptive diseases," which means veterans with these conditions are eligible for benefits even though no positive connections to their service can be proven.

The herbicide called Agent Orange contained a dangerous chemical contaminant called dioxin. More than 12.1 million gallons of Agent Orange were used in Vietnam from 1962 through 1970, according to the Aspen Institute, a nonprofit, nonpartisan think tank. An additional 7.4 million gallons of other toxins—Agents White, Blue, Purple, Pink and Green—were also sprayed, exposing our military men and women and three million Vietnamese. Controversy around this herbicide and its effects has persisted for four decades.

In 1964 I knew little about defoliants, though. Bernie was in Okinawa, after all, and his absence was my chance to see how I could manage on my own for three months. He wasn't in the war, but it seemed from his letters that Bernie's squadron was testing the F-4s' performance in preparation for war. Flying at supersonic speeds had its dangers. This deployment was notable, not only for the *Tampa Tribune* but for Bernie. When a letter arrived from him, it took center stage.

> We landed at Naha on Friday the 16th. The squadron we're replacing had some dressed up local girls from the club waiting with a bottle of champagne (French 75). I had 3 glasses and before I got 2 feet away from the airplane, I really felt them after sitting for 11 hours strapped to that hard, hard seat.

The *Tribune* didn't mention the pretty girls and champagne, but I could picture it. The paper did note that the Triple Nickel squadron was engaged in a variety of missions to deploy the F-4s around the world. This was an important one. The pilots flew at supersonic (Mach 1.3) speeds. The fighter interceptors were new and flying farther distances than any fighter had ever flown, even counting mid-air refueling.

> It was quite a trip over. The flight out of Hickam was really hairy. We took off with our tankers (refuelers-KC-135s). A tanker would line up on the runway with the F-4s behind it. The tanker would roll and 45 seconds later the fighters would roll.

The trip to Naha Air Force Base in Okinawa had two legs, each longer than nine hours. The jets and twelve KC-135 jet tankers landed at Hickam Field, Hawaii, after a non-stop 4,750-mile flight from Florida. The planes flew the remaining 5,102 miles to Okinawa the next day, averaging ten hours and fifteen minutes, an exhausting stint that taxed the pilots.

The fourth and last refueling was made in extremely heavy weather. A typhoon had developed:

> The weather was so bad, we couldn't see the other end of the runway. We caught the tanker with one F-4 on each wing and were in solid thunderstorms for ½ an hour, then it was clear until Guam. We had to find other

tankers and go down to 10,000 feet to do our refueling. It was quite an experience, but don't worry, we were not at any time unsafe—I guess it was just my baptism as far as weather is concerned.

The long trip also was a test of the two-man cockpit in fighter planes. The cockpit was a tight squeeze. The pilots endured an uncomfortable position without relief. Having a second pilot gave the first a respite from flying. They all persevered, proving the new cockpits a success.

After the 555th returned from Okinawa, in March of 1965, headquarters turned a three-squadron wing into a four-squadron wing. To even out their pilot strength, they transferred some 555th pilots to the new 557th. In the move several senior guys in the back seat were upgraded to aircraft commanders. That was when Bernie and Jim became part of the 557th Squadron.

Wally and the 555th were assigned to the Udorn Royal Thai Air Force Base in Thailand, where they scored enough aerial victories against the Russian made MiG-21s to be called the first "Ace" squadron in Southeast Asia.

A few months after the merge, in November 1965, the 557th went to Vietnam.

Chapter 3

GOODBYE OKINAWA, HELLO MR. X

During Bernie's three-month deployment in Okinawa, when we lived eight thousand miles apart, his letters eased the separation and kept us together. We penned our longings for each other underneath humor, innuendo, and the details of our daily duties. Those details were like a never ending "to-do" list. I took notes.

Bernie wrote about how much oil to order for the wall heater, asked if the car license plates had expired, and instructed on how to get new ones if they had. He explained how to fix the back door with a nail and punch, "kind of an ice pick thing," and asked me to look for bugs in the lawn. *Bugs?* He wanted to know: How did the kitchen light do? Is Lisa potty-trained yet? Does she talk very much, and what does she say?

The German genes were working overtime. I realized how lucky I was to be married to this man who wanted everything to work in perfect order. If he expected me to assume command, I would because I loved him and didn't want to fail him.

Bernie always offered a view of Okinawa and his mission there, and I always answered the same way. Careful not to show any weakness that would worry him, I wrote that things were humming at home. Being an air force wife brought out the best in me. Every time I solved a problem I felt lifted to a new level of self-confidence. In fending for myself, I was really fending for the two of us and our daughter—in essence, our marriage.

Our three-month separation was a gentle prelude to Bernie's later deployment to Vietnam. On Okinawa the pilots had practiced electronic countermeasures against our bomber crews to prepare for outsmarting the enemy in a real war situation. I called these tests "war games."

The living conditions at Naha were standard and, at five dollars a week, the maid service was cheap. Bernie paid the maid a whopping eight dollars extra to do his laundry. She even ironed his flight suits, a task he'd never see me do. With only one TV station showing six-month-old sitcoms, the pilots spent their free time shopping for their wives in Naha's boutiques and entertaining themselves with golf and high-stakes card games.

Bernie and Wally land the first F-4 at Naha, Okinawa 1964.

Thousands of military men and their wives were permanently stationed on the island. Wives add civility to any outpost, but that didn't help the men of the 555th.

"I wish the guys here wouldn't bring their wives to the club because it sure reminds me of you," Bernie wrote. "In other words, I miss you, and the *Playboy* magazines in the alert shack don't help."

I bundled the letters with a ribbon and stowed them in a dresser drawer. They piled up on my nightstand until the day Bernie returned in March 1965. He eagerly accepted his hectic schedule at MacDill and I busied myself with our daughter, Lisa. With the squadron reunited, we caught up with our friends, sharing dinners at the club and the latest gossip about future assignments.

Two months later my mother, Patty Palmer, died suddenly of a brain aneurysm. She was fifty-four. I was incredulous, but Bernie knew what had to be done. He took leave and arranged our flight to Chicago, where Rudy and Gretel met us at O'Hare and took Lisa into their care while we went to Saint Louis.

My mother was one of those rare personalities who, in her own sincere and unpretentious way, radiated warmth and understanding toward others. Mother, who'd been executive director of the American Heart Association in Saint Louis, had just been installed as president of the Saint Louis chapter of the Business and Professional Women's Clubs of America. The visitors and phone calls to my parents' apartment never seemed to end.

As Bernie and I walked in, my dad, sister, and aunts stood in the bedroom, discussing funeral arrangements. I felt the grief-filled tension immediately, as if a dark curtain had descended. *So this is what tragedy feels like.* I wanted to go back to last Christmas when Mother and I talked past midnight on the bedroom porch over toasted cheese sandwiches and gin and tonics. Patty adored Bernie, and the feeling was mutual. When he flew overnights to Saint Louis to pick up a new F-4 from McDonnell Aircraft, Mother took him out for drinks and dinner at one of her favorite restaurants.

The crush of people at the wake, all wanting a word with the survivors, made me want to withdraw to the lounge in the back. I thought of my 1956 copy of the *Air Force Wife Manual*, which said a wife should be prepared to handle death with grace and aplomb: "A morbid preoccupation with one's own tragedy is as distressing to others as callous flippancy." I cried in private, with Bernie at my side.

I pushed my sadness inward and, during the next two days, took the lead on how to comport myself from my aunts who told stories about growing up in a boisterous family of nine girls. I didn't consider their musings "callous flippancy." They were our survival mechanism. Laughter lightened the load. The stories revived my mother's past and became a precious gift in themselves that grew with the sharing.

Patty told me her own tales as I was growing up. They all came to mind, complete with her hand gestures and uproarious laughter. When I was in my early teens, Mother gave me the diary she had kept at sixteen, along with an empty one for me, which I filled up with my own stories and code words—in case they reached the wrong hands.

Thoughts of my mother filled my mind even after we returned to Florida. One summer afternoon before Bernie left for Vietnam, a Tampa police detective came by and asked us to help him find out more about our new next-door neighbors. I'd found them standoffish and hadn't even attempted an introduction. The detective said our neighbor was a professional burglar who'd been convicted twice. Under Florida law a third arrest and felony conviction would mean a life sentence.

"Whoa," Bernard said.

"You can't be serious!" I squeaked. "Why would they move into this neighborhood, so close to MacDill Air Force Base with all these small Ranch houses?"

Detective Flynn explained the burglar and his wife and child were Cuban.

"You can call him Mr. X," Flynn said. "He has another wife and child in the Cuban community on the other side of town. Your white, middle-class world is his cover. He thinks he'll be invisible here.

46

"Mr. X wears an expensive suit and tie, takes his briefcase, drives to Tampa Airport, and flies to Miami to pull off his heists," the detective continued. "He wants to look like an important businessman. We at the department think you folks can be trusted to help us."

"You mean trusted to spy?" I asked.

"Yes, in so many words, that's it, ma'am."

We were sitting in our living room. I saw the car parked outside didn't have "Police" painted on it and I was glad — plain clothes, plain sedan.

Sergeant Flynn showed his credentials to Bernie, who then passed them to me. I looked them over carefully as if I knew the difference between a counterfeit and the genuine article.

"It's okay," my husband assured me. "He's for real."

Detective Flynn explained that he had looked up Lieutenant Giere's security clearance and commendations. He offered to watch our house and car, especially when Bernie was away. It made me feel safe to know Detective Flynn would look after me.

"Mr. X never carries a gun," he said, "and he wouldn't have one in the house.

"Phew," I said. "At least he won't shoot me."

Flynn and Bernie chuckled nervously. This assignment sounded legitimate, not like the spying episodes I carried on as a kid— my antidote for boredom in a neighborhood with no other kids. The Stantons never knew I hid under their front porch and listened to their after-dinner conversations. Their brawny sons spilled out tough words I stored away for future examination.

We agreed to help Flynn, who was working with the FBI, and call him if we had a lead. My pilot was soon facing two long trips, so Lisa and I would be alone. I hoped I could pull off this spy caper against Mr. X with dignity and not give myself away.

I had not introduced myself to these new neighbors, other than to nod and exchange a few pleasantries over the back fence. They kept to themselves. Now I knew why and I wondered if I would have the nerve to speak to them again. And how could I keep my eye on them and look for license plate numbers or strange cars or activities?

Our best view of Mr. X's carport was from the high, narrow window in our utility room behind our carport. I rigged up a stack of sturdy boxes so I could peer out through that window and take notes.

"What if they see you?" Bernie said.

"Why would they be looking at our carport? I'll be discreet."

"This isn't an episode from *Mission Impossible*, honey. You're dealing with criminals, you know." He threw up his hands and smiled. "We'll see."

One summer evening as we sat with Lisa on the front porch, we noticed lots of cars parking in front of our notorious neighbor's house. Salsa music blared, which was unusual, and bongo drums were set up next to tables and chairs in their carport. Party guests headed for the house.

"It's time for a walk, don't you think?" I said, persuading Bernie to find Lisa's stroller. Fifteen minutes later, we plopped her in and walked her along the sidewalk, while I copied down license plate numbers with a tiny pencil on a scrap of paper I tucked around the stroller handle. No one seemed to notice or care about us as the party continued.

Another call to Flynn prompted a surreptitious midnight meeting between him and Bernard at a 7-Eleven store five blocks away. He accepted my list with gratitude.

After that episode, Bernie's upcoming trip preempted more spying. The squadron was leaving for a deployment in Southeast Asia—defense duty, the *Tampa Tribune* wrote. Every reader would know we wives were on our own for the duration, but no one was supposed to know where our husbands were.

Chapter 4

OFF TO WAR

Everything was soggy that night in Tampa when we pulled up to the MacDill Air Force Base flight line. A big plane revved up.

"That's our taxi, Old Shaky," said Bernie, pointing to the C-124 transport. "But don't worry, honey. Each of those four engines generates about 3,800 horsepower, so you can be sure we'll get there in one piece."

The behemoth was waiting to transport my husband and the other pilots of the 557th Tactical Fighter Squadron to the South Vietnamese Air Force Base at Cam Ranh Bay on the South China Sea.

These F-4C Phantom fighter pilots of the 12th Tactical Fighter Wing would be the first to update the old airstrip on the sand into a modern air base. Runways were being laid, barriers to protect the aircraft created, and Quonset huts dressed up for pilots' quarters. For eight years, until the conflict ended, the base would serve as a staging point for planes flying missions in South and North Vietnam. But that night Bernard and I didn't question how long the war would last; that would come later.

The pilots had twenty minutes before takeoff when we ducked into the Flight Line Café where the men and their wives occupied every table. The jukebox boomed out the We Five rendition of "You Were On My Mind." I felt uncomfortably adrift on the waves of all the smoke. The colonel had passed out cigars that morning. I chuckled when I saw a few nonsmokers playing at smoking. Those fighter pilots must have thought their cigars signified something— perhaps notoriety for being in the first unit to arrive at Cam Ranh Bay?

All these fliers, most not yet thirty, were going to test their mettle at last. After a year at MacDill Air Force Base, they had become such a tight group that even their nicknames took on a greater significance. In pilot training Bernard's flight instructor sat with his trainees around him. When he called on twenty-four-year-old Giere, he said, "Bernard? Huh. That name will get in the way. How 'bout Ben?" The name stuck.

Bernie and his F-4 Phantom.

Jim and Sandi, sitting next to the window, motioned for us to join them. Outside the rain drummed on as we made our way to them, past couples leaning across tables, holding hands, and speaking in low tones as if sharing secrets. I was relieved to sit down.

"Ben, this is the best stogie I've ever had," Jim said. I remembered I'd left Bernie's in the car. When I offered to get it, he held me back with a smile.

"Forget it, honey," he quipped. "I'll get it later."

Jim passed his cigar over.

"Take a drag of this," he insisted. Ben accepted. After Bernie was upgraded to aircraft commander, Jim would be his copilot, or Guy in the Back Seat, for the rest of their tour. Their friendship had been cemented a year earlier when they were deployed in Okinawa for three months.

From the way Jim and Bernard talked, the three-day ride to Cam Ranh Bay was going to be the worst part of their twelve-month tour. There'd be no first class or stewardesses on Old Shaky.

"Please, ladies," we'd been told, "the colonel says not to divulge our destination to anyone. It's a military secret."

We were supposed to say, "He's been deployed to Southeast Asia."

And oh yes, Sandi and I each had a two-year old daughter to keep us company. Both Lisa and Christy were to be big sisters in six months' time.

"I'm going to call my son Jamie," Jim said. *How presumptuous!*

"How can you be so sure it will be a boy?" I asked.

"Sandi and I worked it out," he boasted. "Didn't we, Sandi?"

I thought it was impossible to work out a baby's sex in advance. Four of us squadron wives were pregnant. The only predictor we ever talked about was the silly needle on a string game, and that was only a fortune teller's ploy. I turned to Sandi for their secret.

"I'll tell you later," she mouthed.

After hearing Jim's announcement, Bernie's face lit up with a grin.

51

"I have no preference, really," he said, "as long as it's healthy."

He put his hand around my shoulder and gave it a squeeze. That sweet touch radiated through me and filled me with pride. I knew he was telling the truth. Had there ever been a more thoughtful husband?

I looked through the windowpane at the wavy silhouettes of airmen loading duffel bags onto a plane. Ten minutes to go.

Our table conversation seemed inconsequential, just words lost in the air. I prattled on, merely dancing around The Fear—the fear of separation, of his capture, of his death, of widowhood. Fear of that day when a blue staff car would pull into my driveway and the base chaplain and grievance officer would ring the bell.

That very drama had recently happened to my neighbor, Nancy. Her husband had been one of the first Forward Air Controllers (FACs) sent to Vietnam. FACs flew small, commercial-type airplanes over the treetops, scouted for targets, and then relayed their positions to the F-4s, which were above them and poised to strike. (Bernard had been to FAC training that summer, even though his position as an F-4 pilot was secure. He never refused an opportunity to master something new.) As Nancy arrived home with her three little boys and a trunk full of groceries, she saw that bold blue staff car in her driveway.

The official word of Coz's death came from the commander's wife. I took the lead from her on when to visit and what to bring. I didn't know what to say to Nancy, or if my voice would hold up through my tears. Somehow I got through it and the funeral that followed.

After that the vulnerability of a pilot's life became a reality that helped define my role in this new war experience. My friends from the past, who carried on their civilian lives as if there were no Vietnam, seemed disconnected, foreign. I thought of Bernard as Teddy Roosevelt would have: "The credit belongs to the man who is actually in the arena … who strives valiantly."

The café door opened suddenly. The loadmaster waddled in, his boots puddling the linoleum. He grabbed the nearest coffee cup and gulped it.

"Let's go!" he shouted. "Now or never."

Bernard shouldered his bag and we left the café. With his hand around my waist, he steered me to a private spot near the runway gate. The rain was lessening. The wing tip lights blinked. Too soon, the pilots began peeling away from their wives and heading toward the plane. Bernard pulled me to him.

"I love you, honey," he said. "Everything's gonna be alright. My mother will fly down to help you when the baby comes."

His embrace never felt as precious—strong, familiar, comforting. I wanted to say something substantial, some words of reassurance, but I couldn't.

"Write soon," I said. "I love you. Be safe."

When I squeezed back into the car and noticed the dark shape on the dashboard, I lost it. *Oh, oh, I forgot to give him his cigar. Oh honey, I'm sorry.* While some wives stood watching Old Shaky take off, I sat in the car groping for something to catch my tears. I drove slowly toward home, not wanting to spoil the memory of us together.

By the end of the week, the realization had set in. I knew this drama wouldn't have a pat ending like an old war movie. I figured that if I could make it until November 1966, Bernard's date of return, I could survive anything.

PART 2

*"Courage is rightly esteemed the first of human qualities...
because it is the quality which guarantees all others."*

— Winston Churchill

Chapter 5

WIVES TOGETHER

Sandi and I joined the new group of squadron wives at Thanksgiving Day dinner. We and our children filled the Officers Club with a spirit of comaraderie. Meanwhile, at Cam Ranh Bay in South Vietnam, our pilots enjoyed a celebration of their own.

General William Westmoreland blessed a hearty Thanksgiving meal for them and wrote this message for their meal:

> This Thanksgiving Day we find ourselves in a foreign land assisting in the defense of the rights of free men everywhere. On this day, we should offer our thanks for the abundant life which we and our loved ones have been provided. May we each pray for His continued blessings and guidance upon our endeavors to assist the Vietnamese people in their struggle to attain an everlasting peace within a free society.

The general topped it off with a prayer to "our almighty and merciful God."

I was glad Bernie sent me the program and to know they'd prayed. He wrote:

> Dear Sarajane and Lisa,
>
> I am no longer a virgin. I got my first combat mission

> today… for lunch we had the Thanksgiving special: turkey, ham, etc. …We go through a line with our mess tins and we have to pay for each meal. 23 cents for breakfast, 50 for lunch and 40 for supper.

We wives shared news of the base at Cam Ranh, an unfortified and undignified strip in the sand. I wondered how safe it was there, knowing how exposed they must be, but Bernard reassured me:

> Our base is guarded by the South Korean Marines—ROKS (Republic of Korea Soldiers). A story is going around that the V.C. captured and slit the throats of 3 ROK officers and the Koreans got angry and found some VC and skinned them alive; consequently, this is the only base in the country that has not been attacked.

I was glad to know he was safe, at least on the ground. I knew Bernard did not mince words. I always told him I wanted the truth. There it was, unvarnished and horrifying. In his vertical, sketchy handwriting, I would get more details as the months went on, always juxtaposed with tender, heartfelt thoughts and his hopes and plans for our future. This first letter ran like a movie in my mind:

> Our combat mission went as follows: took off after getting intelligence, weather and flight briefings. Made several channel changes and contacted a FAC (Forward Air Controller) who is flying in a light spotter plane. He shoots a small colored smoke rocket at the target and he tells us what the army wants hit in relation to the smoke. Most of our missions have been to support the 1st Cavalry. Today we hit a target along a river with bombs and a Gatling Gun.

As I sank down into my favorite living room chair, ready to reread Bernie's letter, I pictured him in his green flight suit, wearing his 557th red baseball cap, and I wondered if he saw me as clearly when he read my letters. As I took in his detailed description of his new home, I saw it in my mind's eye:

> We are living in an awfully crowded Quonset hut, and we have pipe clothes racks. We use wooden ammo boxes for shelves and dressers. The latrine (outhouse) is still up the road a piece, and the showers are well water, unheated. Eventually we're supposed to have showers in the building.
>
> I'll write more later, tired.
>
> Love, Bernard

It wouldn't be long before Bernie would have his wooden crates arranged to maximum usage, as would any man raised by German parents. I knew his roommates must have been grateful and amazed. Good old Bernie could make lemonade out of any lemon.

When the pilots read what syndicated columnist Drew Pearson wrote about Cam Ranh in his column, *Washington Merry-Go-Round*, they were furious. They'd begun building their Officers Club in the sand by laying concrete, scavenging for leftover wood, and doing the construction themselves. Pearson wrote they lived a life of taxpayer luxury and enjoyed a rich and excessive officers club! As time went on, I realized Pearson was one of many who misrepresented the war conditions to their political advantage.

I prayed for my pilot and kept his letters by my bed. I conjured up his voice from behind each sentence. Bernard lived daily in me, as

Bernie next to his F-4, wearing his 557th cap.

I played my role as air force wife. I wasn't going to share these latest gory details about the ROKS with anyone else. Certainly not after hearing what one wife had to say the day I hosted my first wives' coffee.

I first noticed her in the corner of my living room. The other wives seemed drawn to each other. Though I saw her sitting alone, I didn't go over to talk to her. I focused on being a hostess.

Later I heard that she'd asked a gal, "Have you bought your black dress yet?"

"What do you mean by that?" the gal had asked.

"You're all going to need one," the lone wife had replied, "because they're all going to die!"

That conversation stayed with me: *They're all going to die.* I asked myself why I didn't engage her in conversation. Could I have found out more about her? Could I have helped her in some way?

I never found out. Not long after that, she was found dead in her bed. MacDill Base Ops called Cam Ranh and her pilot came home on emergency leave. I was horrified. *This shouldn't have happened. We women are supposed to stick together and help each other.* It was apparent this air force wife needed someone to talk to. She seemed depressed.

Her husband arrived. A short service took place later. The atmosphere of the wake cast a pall over me. No one mentioned the cause of death.

"Perhaps her husband should never have gone to Vietnam," someone said.

That year my survival became a milepost for my future journeys through life. In other words, I grew up.

There were happy occasions, too, for the wives of the 557th. We held a baby shower for all four of us expectant mothers. The celebration was one to remember. The gift I loved the most was a month of diaper service! Washing diapers and standing in the Florida sun to hang them up to dry was my least favorite task. What a boon to have the truck drive up to my house, take my dirty diaper container, and hand me a package of neatly folded ones, ready to go.

The squadron commander's wife invited us all to her house on Easter. I enjoyed watching her brood of children helping with the younger kids.

"How do you manage without your husband here?" I asked.

"Remember this," she replied, "the bigger they are, the bigger the problems."

I knew then that she was right, that two little children were a cinch compared to having older kids. I felt naïve even to have asked her. What a grand gal she was, though. As the war dragged on, I realized how prescient her advice was. I don't know how I would have handled teenagers during the war years that followed and those frantic anti-war demonstration days. How would I have fielded emotional questions about the "unjust war" their father was part of?

I busied myself, remembering what my wives' manual advised: "…Keeping busy serves as a defense or buffer against tension." I'd already attended three funerals and mentally prepared for whatever else was to come.

I put Lisa in the base nursery at one point and took painting lessons from the flight surgeon's wife, a professional artist, which gave me a focus beyond the base. I also attended a Presbyterian church in downtown Tampa that had a lovely nursery for Lisa and a women's Bible study group. I wrote letters, discovered new playgrounds with Lisa, made curtains, knitted, played bridge, and prepared for the baby.

Chapter 6

GETAWAY

Young Bernie (center) with his brother and parents, Rudy and Gretel.

Lisa and I flew to Chicago to see Rudy and Gretel for the Christmas holiday. A snowstorm prevented us from landing at O'Hare. We ended up in Milwaukee and took a bus down to O'Hare. How relieved I was to see Oma and Opa waiting for us. We settled in for a few days, and on Christmas Eve drove back to O'Hare to pick up my dad, John, who was grateful to be with us. Living alone for the first time in thirty-four years, Daddy was still in grief. He soothed his depression with cocktails, which embarrassed me, but there wasn't much I could do. Rudy and Gretel understood.

We all turned our attention to Lisa, who was fascinated with the lovely Christmas tree and all the gifts under it. The gory battle news from the war front poured forth from the TV in the living room. We didn't watch Walter Cronkite and the six o'clock news as much as I wanted to, though. The Gieres turned off the TV and served dinner promptly at six. Most nights I watched the late news after my in-laws went to bed.

When Andy Williams televised his Christmas special, we gathered to watch. His beautiful French wife, daughter, and baby son joined Andy in a living-room setting to celebrate Christmas. Surrounded by a chorus of beautiful people, Andy sang to a full orchestra. It tore me apart. I thought, *I should be sitting here with Bernie and our children instead of the safe and sound Williams family.* Would we ever be together again like they were? My poor dad was the loneliest of all that night. I backed into the dining room to shed my tears, wishing it were next Christmas.

Every letter that came direct from Cam Ranh was a special event. Bernard raved about his mother's food packages. He hosted a cocktail hour for the guys in his section, serving her sardines, cheese, and Westphalian Rye to go with the drinks. Gretel looked forward to her son's thank you letters. She saved them all, just like I saved mine. She didn't like to write. Her letters were food packages, which said more than any letter could.

Bernard also had written that the 557th Squadron Christmas tree looked good. It was made of beer can pull tabs, chained together, and thin strips of toilet paper.

> We went to church Christmas Eve and afterwards the squadron had a steak fry in the mess tent. We all had 24 hours to make a gift for a name we drew, and then Claude Kincaid came in as Santa, dressed in a red cardboard hat and poncho. He ended up looking much like the Phantom, tennis shoes and all.

All my love to everyone, and hugs and kisses for the Giere girls.

Love, Bernard

Bernie and the guys enjoying some down time while at Cam Ranh.

Rudolf and Gretel brought out their Christmas tree tin candle-holders. They were sturdy little guys that slid onto the branches like clothespins. Rudy lit the candles on Christmas Eve, but only for a little while. *It's magical*, I thought, *as it might have been when Bernie was a boy.*

We looked forward to seeing the *Bob Hope Christmas Special* from Cam Ranh, which Bernie said would be aired January 19th:

> You must see it. Try to see it in color. There were about 7000 guys there all dressed in green. We are sitting on the side of a hill holding a red, 557th flag, with our red baseball hats on. I was sitting to the right of the flag, two or three people to the right, and I do have a semblance of a mustache...I started growing it on Dec. 1.
> Before the show we presented a squadron hat to Hope and he wore it during the show. He said the 557th

flag would look good on his Chrysler. I met Hope and Jerry Colonna and shook their hands—Colonna commented on my mustache.

When the show appeared in the Giere living room, we barely made out the red hats in the background. Bob Hope was donning the red cap, though, and Jerry Colonna clowned around during the skits. He was known for his handlebar mustache, and as time went on, Bernie was known for his, too.

I treasured my letters, even the ones containing bad news, as one we received in early December:

9 Dec. 1965

Dear Sarajane, Mom and Dad,

It is now 0700 and I am sitting around the ops (operations) shack with my G suit, water wings, holster and .38 combat master piece pistol, a radio strapped to my stomach, my harness on, and my helmet and checklist close at hand. As you might guess, I am sitting alert until noon, when I am scheduled for a mission.

Two days ago, on the morning of 7 December, we left a flight of three F-4s and returned as a flight of two. James Sala and Wayne Warnosky were lead, Joe Tuck and I were 2 and Joe Fidler and Jerry Daniel were 3. Sala and Warnosky started a dive bomb run on a target on a 3,300-foot hill. Two bombs hit near the target, but their F-4 hit the ground ½ mile away, and there was a large red fireball laced with dense black smoke.

We landed one hour and fifty minutes later. As we were getting into the truck to go to debriefing, an Airman 1st, by the name of Holly, came up with a quizzical look and asked, "Seven two three...Seven two three... where is seven two three?" That was the tail number of the plane that crashed—the one that Holly, a crew chief, took care of. Daniel mentioned something about being "in the woods," and our truck started to roll.

That short exchange and the helpless feeling of seeing James and Wayne crash I'll never forget. It could have been ground fire or even a heart attack. We'll never know. They were listed as KIA (killed in action).

That is all I can say for now, and don't worry one inch about the kid here. I'll do my damnedest to fly safely and keep out of anybody's sights.

All my love to you all, I miss you—

Bernard

Gretel with Lisa and Paul.

I sank when I read this. My heart ached for my pilot and Bernie's parents, too, who hid their anxieties for my sake. I knew the 557th was a tight group and that this tragedy—happening so soon after their arrival—must have felt like a precursor of what was to come. How glum it must have been in the debriefing room and afterwards.

It seemed bad news was creeping closer to me. Watching a TV reporter rattle the weekly death tolls was nothing like hearing it firsthand from Bernie, who watched his flight mates disappear into a red fireball.

Angels have a way of manifesting themselves when they're needed most and I found mine on Christmas Eve at the Giere house. The night was particularly cold. When all were asleep, I rooted in Oma's kitchen for a sweet snack. I didn't think Gretel would notice my high-calorie theft from her cookie tins on the cold-porch. The phone rang. I grabbed the receiver from the wall phone and heard a woman's voice say, "Is this Sarajane speaking?"

"Yes," I answered. "Who's this?"

"It's the operator. I have a call on the line for you."

Then I heard Bernard's voice, crackly and distant. "Hi, honey, it's me, your husband."

I sank to the floor. *This can't be.*

"Hey honey, are you there?"

Say something.

"Yes," I mumbled, my eyes filling with tears.

"How ya doin', hon, and how's Lisa?"

I wonder if he is all right. I wanted to ask him, but the words wouldn't come.

"Can you hear me?" Bernard asked again. "How are you?"

He wants to know how we are.

"I'm… I'm—" I choked.

Bert, my angel operator, took over for me.

"Are you okay?" she asked me.

"Yes," I whispered.

"She's fine, Ben, and she says your daughter's fine, too."

I tasted my salty tears and felt my legs shiver against the icy linoleum.

"That's good and don't worry about me," Bernie said. "I'm fine here, honey."

I thought of Warnosky and Sala who had been killed two weeks earlier. I wanted to believe him.

"Sarajane says she won't worry," Bert said.

"I love you, honey," Ben said. I wanted to reply but I was sobbing like a baby. I heard static on the line, eight thousand miles of it.

"He loves you," Bert said. "Do you love him?"

"Yes," I squeaked.

"She loves you, Ben."

"Tell her I love her, too," he said.

"He loves you, too," Bert said, adding that Bernard's time was up. Others were waiting.

"Goodbye, honey," I said. "Write soon. I love you." He said he'd try to call me again and repeated that I shouldn't worry. I managed to thank Bert through my tears.

"My pleasure," she said. "We'll call another time."

Bert Pratt worked as a telephone operator at a California military base. Her sympathetic ear earned her a reputation among the pilots as their lifeline to home. She was their California Cupid who took chances by arranging our conversations at night, so they wouldn't interfere with her official military duties during the day.

Bert called many more times. Bernie wrote on Jan. 9th, "I sure love you and miss you, and it brings you to mind when I get to talk, or almost talk, with you."

During that long year, through happy and tragic occasions, Bert got to know us and our voices. We wives never forgot her kindness. Neither did our husbands. When the pilots of the 557th returned, they tracked her down and presented her with a string of pearls.

Many years later during a reunion, one of the pilots said he'd heard a rumor that our Bert had been fired because of those clandestine calls. Some said it wasn't true. What happened to her, no one knew.

Bert gave me the best Christmas gift ever—kindness, sympathy, and reassurance. Aside from the birth of our son the following May, hearing my pilot's voice for the first time since we'd parted was the highlight of my Vietnam year. For a few, frosty minutes on Oma's back porch, I became one step closer to having Bernie in my arms again.

My pilot talked more through his letters than he did on the phone. He talked about our future and what he hoped to do when his commitment was up in two years: should he stay in the service, or get out and try for an airline job?

> I'm thinking more and more about getting out because I can see myself as a 35-year-old major, playing the same game of PCS [permanent change of station] and TDY [temporary duty yonder]. In other words, we'd always be moving to a new base, and I would constantly be away from home. I love you and Lisa too much.
>
> I guess Grandpa is doing an outstanding job with Lisa—that little tiger sure does need a man to keep her in line, she is a great roughhouser. Keep up the good work, Opa—but don't spoil her more than she is.

Lisa and I bid the Gieres goodbye the day after New Year's Day. We flew to LaGuardia Airport in New York where we met Germaine and her husband, Tom, who lived in an apartment in Queens. Since we had kids the same age, my sister and I had more in common. Though John was three months older than Lisa, she matched him jump for jump. Ten-month-old Paula became Lisa's living doll. I loved being with my big sister. Germaine, who'd flown around the world as a TWA stewardess, and seemed just as comfortable in New York City as back home in Saint Louis.

Bernie, who always knew where we were, started addressing his letters to us in New York. My letters back were full of advice I'd gleaned about the airlines. Figuring out the future was a way to get through such a tense time. Germaine heard TWA and Pan Am were eager to hire pilots with military experience. It was heady to think Bernard had qualifications that would shape our future. Plus, the opportunity for travel was enticing. I tried not to get too excited because we'd recently heard President Lyndon Johnson inaugural address: he said the US would stay in Vietnam until the aggression had stopped. Would Bernard return only to go back the next year? That was the talk among the fellows in the 557th.

One night I watched the kids while Tom and Germaine were out with friends. Germaine gave me the number of her friend who lived downstairs, just in case I needed anything. She also left the name of the restaurant they were going to. The kids fell asleep. I delved into a book that made the next few hours tick by like minutes. It was a story about two young men who savagely murdered a farm family of four in the middle of Kansas—*In Cold Blood* by Truman Capote. I heard a rap at the door. *Who could be knocking at this hour?* I shivered and put the book down.

I looked through the peephole of the door, which had three locks. A young man stood on the other side.

"What on earth are you doing here this time of night?" I asked.

"I'm an encyclopedia salesman," he replied. He looked too young and too casually dressed to be a salesman. *Oh, shit! Heaven help me.*

"I'm not interested," I said. He didn't leave. I called Germaine's downstairs friend.

"There's a strange man knocking at the door," I said. "What do I do now?"

"Joe's coming up. Keep the door locked."

I circled the living room, checked on the kids, and circled some more. I looked through the peephole. The man had disappeared. When I heard Joe bounding up the stairs at the end of the hallway, I wanted to shout, "Hallelujah!"

"I just saw a man leaving the building," Joe said. "Open the door, and don't worry." He came in. "Are you alright?"

Minutes later his wife, Joan, appeared. They calmed me down. I made us all drinks for the conversation that followed. Joe called the super of the building, who told him a few incidents like this had happened before. *How comforting*, I thought. *Phew! Welcome to the big city, Sarajane.*

After the neighbors left, I said a prayer of gratitude, calmed down, poured another drink, put my feet up, and turned on the *Tonight Show*. Johnny Carson was interviewing Truman Capote, who was plugging his new best seller, *In Cold Blood*.

When Germaine and Tom came home, they digested my news with alarm. Tom was a New York City policeman. He plied me with questions about this incident and Mr. X. in Tampa. Tom told me to be careful in Tampa and not tell the neighbors I was taking notes about Mr. X. When I told him Sergeant Flynn was looking after me, he seemed impressed. As for the punk at the door, he said not to worry.

I read Bernie's Christmas letter to Germaine and Tom. We watched the repeat of the *Bob Hope Christmas Special*, took the kids into the city, and filled our days and nights with each other. We were preoccupied with the children—a distracting but entertaining way to attend to the present instead of ruminating about the future.

Lisa and I returned home in February. Germaine promised a Tampa visit after the baby was born.

Bernie in Hong Kong.

Chapter 7

BAIL OUT NO. 1 - BABY NO. 2

Jim and Bernie

When Jim and Bernie arrived at Cam Ranh, both were second lieutenants, back-seaters. Jim was paired with another pilot named Bob. They were shot down and rescued in a harrowing episode. Soon afterward, when Bob learned his wife had suddenly died, he returned to Florida. Since Bernie recently had been upgraded to the front seat, filling one of three open command pilot seats, he and Jim paired up. They liked flying together.

Meanwhile, Sandi and I became closer, as did our daughters, who played together happily while we compared our pilots' letters. As our May delivery dates grew closer, Bernie's letters grew more animated.

In his hastily written letter dated May 4th, I learned he and Jim had lost an airplane, bailed out, and were rescued. I took a deep breath and reread it. *Oh, my God. They could have died. Heaven help us.* Bernie told me only what I needed to know, and I was satisfied with that. Better to hear it from him than one of the wives. Our pilots were safe. That's what counted.

Bernie asked me not to tell Sandi until after she delivered on May 8th, four days after the incident happened. It was Jim's second ejection. The odds were against him surviving a third.

Later I found out more details. Upon arriving back at the Cam Ranh runway after a strike mission, the flight of four was coming down on final approach. They were low on fuel. The runway was slick with a downpour—a situation worse than they'd been led to expect. Such a hard rain wasn't unusual during the monsoon season, but it unsettled the ground-controlled approach (GCA) personnel whose radar proved inadequate in rain. As Bernie told it:

> The first plane landed okay, but the controller told me to go around again because a plane ran off the runway. I picked up the gear and flaps, made a missed approach, and remained in the soup at all times. GCA told me to try again, and I followed my flight leader in to land but GCA had him too far to the left and we both made a missed approach.

Bernie told the flying supervisor, his superior, they were at minimum fuel and wanted to divert to nearby Phan Rang Air Base.

"No, you'll land here," the supervisor said.

The rain picked up intensity. Bernie's engines flamed out. He and Jim ejected from the plane, which crashed away from the runway, allowing them to survive the parachute ride down with a salute to the Martin-Baker Ejection Seat.

May 4, 1966

Dearest Darling Sarajane,

It was raining, the visibility was 1/8th of a mile and breaking action on the runway—which is made of aluminum and is like ice under rainy conditions—was about zero. We circled around but ran out of gas. Both engines quit, so we ejected a mile from the runway, and were picked up by helicopters. I was on the ground not more than 3 minutes and sitting in the flight surgeon's office 5 minutes after that.

I am fine, and I love you very much and I hope you are OK now and there is nothing to worry about. It was a long chain of circumstances that could only happen here at Cam Ranh. Don't tell Sandi.

Thinking of you, and always sending love,

Your Bernard

Pilot rescue in Nam.

Only one of four planes in that flight landed normally. Bernie's was in the bay. Two others took cables. This operations decision caused the loss of a plane but not the lives of its pilots. In the days following the incident, the circumstances surrounding the F-4 loss was debated among the hierarchy, which made Jim and Bernie uneasy. Things eventually turned out well.

I thought of my pilot's letter as I went to see Sandi and baby Karen at Saint Joseph's Hospital. It was a Sunday, and Tampa's downtown streets were deserted. I glanced at my profile reflected in a store window and was glad I didn't own a full-length mirror at home. *Yikes! What a blimp.* I wondered how I'd hold out for three more weeks until my baby was due.

My thoughts returned to Bernie's letter. What he didn't say interested me more than what he said. He'd added that he'd shaved off his mustache after the bailout and that he and Jim flew to Clark Air Force Base in the Philippines for R&R (rest and recovery). I was glad of that. They needed downtime. I kept my mouth shut about the ejection.

May 11, 1966

Darling Sarajane,

The rumor is that the line between here and Bert has been found out and cut off somewhere. I think PACAF (Pacific Air Forces) has found us out and if I do not get to talk via Bert, I will call you from Clark in the Philippines. I will not leave here anymore until I find out if it is a Patty or Paul.

Takeoff on the Ticonderoga aircraft carrier.

I couldn't believe they would stop Bert from letting us talk to each other, and I fretted about it. As I discovered later, the rumor was partially true. There was more to the story.

The days crawled by as I awaited my next letter and our baby, who would arrive on May 21st. Bernie's birthday was May 29th.

Bernie's next letter raised both our spirits. He wrote that he'd spent some time on the aircraft carrier, the Ticonderoga. Its arrival gave a lucky air force pilot a chance to go back with the navy flier on their mail plane, called a COD (carrier onboard delivery). After it touched down at the base, three naval officers jumped off and ran to the Officers Club to have some booze.

"None allowed on the ship," Bernie wrote.

My pilot relished the opportunity to return to the carrier with the navy pilot:

> I sat in the copilot's seat and got to fly the plane in for a night landing. The pilot said to hold 105 knots and follow the meatball—an electronic guidance system. We hit the deck and then our hook snared the cable. It was about 10:00 at night.

Landing on a carrier was no easy task, especially at night.

On the Ticonderoga Bernie enjoyed white tablecloths and steaks for dinner, quite an upgrade from the powdered eggs and milk he was used to. The next morning he had breakfast in the officer's mess.

"How would you like your eggs?" the waiter asked.

"I'd like them sunny side up because I want to see them," Bernie said.

The luxury lasted two days. In the meantime, the navy aviators stayed at Cam Ranh. After that, I never heard Bernie joke about navy aviators, as he and his buddies used to do. The navy grew in status in Bernie's mind.

Ten days before his birthday, Bernie wrote:

> May 19, 1966
>
> Dear Girls,
>
> Happy Ho Chi Min's Birthday. I guess all sorts of characters have birthdays in May. I got my birthday package today. The Batman sign is hanging over the door to our room and I am wearing my new slippers. Thanks for everything. Bert called tonight but only two guys got through. Not much new, just waiting for the new tax deduction.
>
> Love, Bernard

Gretel, my sweet mother-in-law, arrived at the Tampa airport the evening of May 20th. Little did we know her grandson would be born the next morning instead of seven days later, on his predicted due date.

Compared to O'Hare, the Tampa airport seemed sleepy with long, tropical outdoor corridors, and skimpy, corrugated roofs to ward off the rain. Lisa flew to the gate like a bird, skipping in her red sandals one minute, dancing the next. Oma was arriving and so was her new baby! After giving the house a fly-by cleaning job that afternoon and installing extra towel racks in the bathroom, I was exhausted. I plodded behind like Tweedledee—a helium balloon with arms, legs, and a lifeless ponytail.

That evening I began labor and was whisked off to Saint Joe's by my wonderful neighbors, Bobby and Mel. I was in labor again, confined to a crib-like bed with no attendants other than a nurse who popped her head in now and then. Finally, the next morning, the doctor came and sped up the birth process, of which I have only a vague memory. I must have screamed my head off because after the delivery, my throat felt like sandpaper.

I was delighted to see my healthy baby boy, whom I named Paul Bernard Giere. Bernie and I had talked about the name Paul but never Bernard; that was my call. He had a bruise on top of his football-shaped head, and long, spindly legs, but his facial features were beautiful.

"He favors his father," Gretel said. "Bernard had a big head, too."

Compared to petite little Lisa, Paul was all boy.

For four days after the birth, Bobby and Mel, my wonderful neighbors, looked after Lisa and Gretel. My daughter had her adoring Oma all to herself. Gretel seized my kitchen like a conquering chef and invited Lisa to help her cook. Bobby drove them both to the hospital to see me and the baby, which cheered me up. Seeing them so happy made Bernie loom even larger in my thoughts. There I was with a darling newborn baby, nurses on call, and my daughter, happy in the arms of her doting grandmother. And there was my lover, risking his life every day in the pressure cooker of war. More anti-war rallies appeared on the TV evening news. I asked my roommate to turn it off.

My hospital room shrunk in size as my roommate's family and friends took over. I wasn't prepared for the sadness I felt whenever this happy clan overstayed the strict visiting hours limit. Commandeering my chairs, they chattered away in Spanish, passed food around, and took enough pictures to fill five scrapbooks. All the while, I tried not to feel sorry for myself—a difficult thing in the midst of this happy crowd, but I made a valiant effort, knowing Bernie would want me to.

Sandi visited and lightened my spirits. Her mom, who'd flown down from Ohio, was watching her girls. We talked about our babies and our pilots. She shook me out of my self-pity. After she left, I realized our loneliness united us with all the other wives whose pilots served abroad. Knowing we were not alone, I eventually found strength and comfort.

Bernie knew he had a boy early on. The baby news traveled like a bullet from one headquarters to another. What a bash that must have been at the Officers Club. I received a letter that looked as if it had been written at the big party. "IT'S A BOY" was scribbled all over the envelope and sentences rode the waves on each page. The next letter made more sense:

> May 23, 1966
>
> Hi All,
>
> The command post called me about 10 p.m. Saturday the 21ˢᵗ, and I guess Paul was born about 5 a.m. I figure I found out just a few hours after he was born. Be sure to fill me in on all the details. Does he have any hair? How did you get to the hospital? The night I got the word I set out a bottle of V.O. and a bottle of Old Grand Dad and they were both gone by 1 a.m. I didn't have any cigars.
>
> I hope you are both okay and healthy. The command post said he is 7 pounds and 15 ounces and that you are both okay and that my mother was there.
>
> I am very happy that you both are okay and that I can buy an electric train for Christmas. Don't get him a baseball or football. Get him a set of golf clubs. That

is a good clean sport and that is where the money is. We will not only perpetuate the Giere name, but he will probably become famous. Who does the little guy look like? Hope Lisa isn't disappointed she has a little brother instead of a sister.

My love and congratulations and thanks to my darling wife.

Love, Your Bernard

That squadron party must have been a corker. Bernie didn't have to buy drinks and those pilots would gamble for anything just to keep their sanity. I didn't want to judge them, even though it pained me to hear they made such a fuss about boys versus girls. Ironically, Bernie seemed to be the only expectant father who didn't state a preference. After I received his "It's a Boy" letter in its drunken script, I realized that most men probably wanted to pass on their name through a son, no matter what they told everyone else.

May 30, 1966

Hi Girls—

I did get the picture of Paul and he looks pretty good. In your last letter, you sounded as if everything was pretty well under control with Paul feeding and sleeping well, Oma cooking, and Lisa pleased to see a brother and coming out with funny comments all day long. Just thinking out loud—maybe you should not let Lisa hold Paul because she might sneak in and pick him up sometime when you are not around. In any case, I think it should be made quite clear that he is not a toy. I do not mean to lecture.

I was beginning to see the German in my husband, and it amused me. He had flown the nest and could no longer preside over us like a good husband and father in control of home and hearth. Peppering his letters with advice and counsel endeared him to me as I soldiered on, trying not to doubt myself too much.

When things turned out well, I piled up the confidence points like A+ report cards. Lisa was talkative and thriving, a great little companion. Baby brother Paul was her captive audience who smiled upon command. Seeing the two of them together gave Grandma Gretel that sense of happiness she needed so badly. She had not only mastered her second airplane ride just to be with us, but now she had two grandchildren to love.

In one short week Gretel had entered a new world, and we were all the better for it. She handled the baby like an expert and knew when to take charge of Lisa when I needed to catch a nap or have time to myself. Gretel, a needlework master, taught me to tame knitting needles and count cross-stitch, which made those long evenings sail along in concert with our conversations. Lisa and I called her Oma and she liked that. Later I realized that if Bernie hadn't been gone during those years, giving Gretel the opportunity to be with me so often, I might never have known her as well or come to love her as I did. I was only forty-two when she died of a stroke at seventy-two.

My initial sadness at losing Bernie for a year morphed into quiet contentment: I had a beautiful, good baby and a darling daughter who was happy with life, especially her new baby brother and her neighborhood playmates.

When Gretel left three weeks after Paul's birth, Lisa felt let down. I was ready to take over and promised Lisa we'd go to Chicago to see her grandparents after her daddy returned. I assured Gretel she could count on our visit. Bernie probably would have at least a week off before he began his flight instructor duties at MacDill.

Future plans were good medicine.

Chapter 8

NIGHT WATCH

Paul awoke twice each night to be nursed. I grew used to the interruption, actually enjoying our time together. We nestled in the plush, living room rocker under my grandma's quilt. Each time I gazed through the picture window, watching for stars above the palm trees, I talked to God, keeping the channel open between us so his power could hold me up and keep me going. I prayed for Bernie and wondered what he was doing at that very moment. I closed my eyes. *What would it feel like to have his arms around me again?*

What would his expression be on seeing Lisa and his new son?

Wrapped up with the warmth of my baby and with Lisa sleeping soundly in her bedroom, I felt grateful, safe, at peace with the night. When a friend asked how it was to have a child without Bernie there, I told her, "Birthing a baby is one thing any woman can do without her man, thank you."

One night, after our second nursing session, I lay Paul down in his crib and headed to bed, feeling sorry for myself. Then I thought of Bernie's letters waiting for me in my nightstand drawer. It was remarkable to see his sentiments bubble up and flow across the page and into my eager hands though he was six thousand miles away. I went right to my last letter and my pilot's closing, which blessed me with a smile:

> My love to you, my sweet, and my thoughts are of you constantly—will you marry me? All my love forever,
>
> Yours, Bernard.

Some nights at the front window, when I held Paul, I liked to rewind the events I'd lived through as if they were unforgettable scenes of a play. I remembered the night a few years earlier when Lisa was a baby and I came down with a bronchial infection that kept me awake and worried. I'd only been a mother for four months, and I was horribly sick. As a new mother, I had my daughter to worry about—not me. Bernie was playing war games at a base in Nevada for the week. Lisa slept soundly in her tiny bedroom. I hacked away in the kitchen, trying not to wake her. I had chills, topped with a fever, sore throat, and a feeling of helplessness. I couldn't leave Lisa by herself. Should I wake her up and head for the base hospital? Saint Joseph's was too far away.

I finally decided to do what my pilot would have wanted me to do. I called our wonderful neighbor, Ed, a friend Bernie trusted.

Ed walked in with a concerned look, saw me, and said, "You're coming with me to the emergency room, Sarajane." Then he called his wife, Barb, to come and watch Lisa. That was the beginning of one of the longest nights I'd ever spent.

Even though we'd only been at MacDill for four months, I saw how different it was from Big Spring, our small pilot training base in West Texas. Thousands of military retirees and their spouses used MacDill's facilities—men and women who were entitled to the same privileges we were, including the hospital and commissary. After all, wasn't this Florida, a haven for retirees of all kinds?

The emergency room was packed that night. Coughing and wheezing became our surround-sound, so I fit right in. No one noticed us. The determined gal at the desk took my husband's name, rank, and serial number, and then listed me as Mrs. Giere. I told her how I was feeling.

"Take a seat and we'll call you," she said.

Ed found us two seats together. He didn't mind if I lay across his lap. As the hours ticked by, Ed went up to inquire about me and returned to our chairs.

"They're waiting for a spot in the X-ray lab," he said.

People came and went through the door. Ed brought me drinks of water and covered me with his jacket. It was then I realized that not all angels are female. Time crawled. Ed pointed out a woman who had just entered—an important general's wife.

"The lady doesn't look sick to me," I groused.

"Hmm, that's hard to say," Ed replied. "You never know."

The sound of my breathing filled my mind with dire predictions. *Bronchitis? Pneumonia?* The two-star wife was called in before I was. *How can they take her before me? I'm dying! I have a baby at home and my husband's somewhere in the Nevada desert.* Ed smiled.

"Waiting your turn around here is par for the course." I sat up. "In other words, I need patience, don't I?"

"In spades," he said, as if amused by my naiveté.

That's easy for you to say, I thought. *You and Bernie were born with it.*

As the morning sun shone through the windows and high-lighted the empty chairs in the emergency room, the technician led me into the X-ray lab for the first chest X-ray I'd ever had. Next, a radiologist had to examine the slides. More patience needed. At last the doctor entered.

"You have a bronchial infection," he said. "Drink plenty of water. Get bed rest, and take aspirin if you need it."

Blessed to have neighbors like Ed and Barb, I recovered quickly. I also learned my lesson well. From then on, I called up Bernie's forbearance when I was in the long, long line at the commissary. Military rules had to be followed even while grocery shopping. For instance, no children were to wander around. If they were old enough, they went to a supervised play area beside the building. If they were Lisa's age, they were strapped in the cart, or else! This was no easy task for my two-year-old daughter, who loved to explore. Also, no one was to carry their own bags to their car; the bag boy did that, and we were to tip him.

I learned the hard way that a big air force base has its own rhythm, too, and if I picked up the beat, life would be easier for me and my lieutenant. I finally realized that MacDill's dictums had been in play since its establishment in 1939. My choice was to op-pose them or accept military life, as Bernie had, and make the best of our situation. I stopped complaining and counted my blessings.

Each night my mind traveled as I nursed Paul from my fa-vorite chair. These moonlight introspections were eclipsed one morning around two when a car pulled into the Jacksons' drive-way across the street. A man got out and entered through the front door. At the next feeding a few hours later, the car was gone. This went on during June and July, a few nights a week. I knew that the husband was in Vietnam or somewhere else overseas and that his wife and infant son were living alone. The car routinely appeared. Always, a man entered and was gone by sunup.

My Lord, what was going on over there? Something was the matter. I wondered why I hadn't walked across the street to get to know them. I wanted to know more, but these midnight visits weren't my business. There I was, probing and spying on a neighbor again.

The next time Bert, our long-distance operator, hooked me up with Bernie, I told him everything. My pilot was supportive. He said there was nothing I could do. For my peace of mind, however, he suggested that I call Detective Flynn since he was looking after me when I was on my own. Why not let him know what I was witnessing? After all, this neighborhood was anything but typical.

I called Flynn. He said he'd check it out and get back to me.

Then I worried if I'd done the right thing. Had I, an officer's spouse, overstepped my bounds? I remembered our commander's wife offering advice from Mamie Eisenhower during WWII: "Ladies, there's not much you can do to help your husbands, but there is a lot you can do to hurt them."

These words echoed back to me during the midnight nursing sessions that followed. I tried to push them away and concentrate on the babe in my arms and the sounds of his ravenous appetite.

I hung on, prayed a lot, and began to see my resiliency for what it was—a propulsion that carried me out of my self-centered, circumscribed, war-wife existence into the dramatic, hidden world right under my nose. Bernie used to tell me I didn't have enough situational awareness. I was certainly aware of what was around me then, maybe too aware.

A week later a call came from a MacDill Air Force Base social worker who seemed familiar with the situation. She suggested it might be a case bordering on child neglect. Child neglect? That hadn't entered my mind.

"Would you attest to seeing the night visitor?" she asked.

"I would like to confer with my husband first," I replied.

I had to protect Lisa and me, especially if this fellow was a predator. What if I didn't come forth? Perhaps I was meant to see what was going on and thus save that baby from a worse fate. Could I say these visits were just those of a certain man, or were the figures different men who looked the same to me in the dark?

I talked to Bernie, then to my brother-in-law, and they both felt I should cooperate with Flynn or the base, if it came to that. The thought of cooperating made me feel both nervous and relieved to have an opportunity to right a wrong. I'd been shaken by the whole business and felt like a naive onlooker. Actually, I was the vulnerable one. I missed Bernie terribly.

As it turned out, I didn't have to appear before the base lawyer or social worker, after all. I welcomed that news. The situation unraveled within the next few weeks. I gathered from Flynn that Sergeant Jackson came home on emergency leave and his mother arrived to take care of the child. The wife left the premises. Flynn didn't say where she went or what happened to her. Soon the father was transferred to a new assignment at another air base.

I gratefully closed that chapter, and found delight in marking off the days, knowing my life would take off again in November when Bernie walked through that door.

Chapter 9

LAY IT RIGHT ON TOP OF US

As President Johnson heightened the conflict and citizens learned more about the devastating effects of napalm and Agent Orange, they spoke out vociferously against the war. Thousands of protesters marched nationwide. Students burned their draft cards. One man, a father of three, doused his body with kerosene and set himself aflame in front of the Pentagon. What exactly was going on? My beloved country was erupting, and my pilot was in the midst of the war causing the upheaval.

I once read that Vietnam had been called the "damnedest, craziest war, ever." When I received Bernie's next letter, dated June 26, 1966, I saw why. It was about an incident that happened the first week of June:

> ...Perry and I were scrambled on an alert flight, he had 500-pound bombs and I had napalm. It was late in the afternoon and we helped—I think—some guys on the ground. You may have heard about the results of that mission. An army captain, Bill Carpenter, West Point football player, had called napalm on himself because he was being overrun by VC. Just before we left the target, the FAC (Forward Air Controller) said, "One of those napalm cans caused some friendly casualties, but you got some VC, too—don't sweat it, they asked

for it." We had to land at Da Nang and there I got sick & could not eat supper. We did some swapping around & I rode back in the back seat that night & got drunk upon return to CRB. After that, Perry & I left for Clark AFB in the Philippines.

The squadron commander, seeing what effect this mission had on Perry and Bernie, sent them to Clark Air Force Base in the Philippines for a few days of R&R. While there, they read about Captain Carpenter in the papers. News traveled fast. The date and place of the action Carpenter described matched the time and location of their napalm drop. Captain Bill Carpenter was a hero.

When Perry and Bernie returned to Cam Ranh, they learned that right after they'd left, the army had sent an officer to thank the pilots who helped Charlie Company, part of the 507th Parachute Infantry Regiment. The officer had assured the squadron leader that no Americans had been killed in the napalm strike.

I put down the letter to gather my thoughts before finishing it. I was relieved Lisa was asleep. I wouldn't have to explain my reaction. I read on:

When we got back to CRB the guys said the army sent a Lt. down here to thank us. That is the end of my tale. I really had to tell you although I did not want to, but I am afraid that that afternoon will be a permanent part of my life, and you are my life also and you and I are one.

I am getting teary eyes and lonesome just thinking about us and our lives together. Sweetheart, I love you very much and I am always thinking of you and our family. Keep up the good work my love & forgive me for not writing sooner.

All my love to you and the children—forever.

Your Bernard

I anguished over how Bernard must have felt when the FAC told him he'd caused some "friendly casualties." I wanted to be there to talk to him, hug him, love him.

Bernie had written that sometimes while they flew bombing runs along the Ho Chi Minh Trail, they were diverted to help the army. This incident was one chilling example. The fact he waited seventeen days to write me about the incident told me he was struggling to digest what he'd done.

Life Magazine Cover,
July 8, 1966
(Life Magazine Archives)

Looking back, I see how the love and support we had for one another mitigated my pilot's emotional ups and downs. I hoped these confessional letters lessened his angst. I welcomed them, grateful I could be his loving confidant half a world away. Our letters collapsed the miles, bringing us closer than we'd ever been.

I saved *Life* magazine's 1966 spread about the Carpenter incident, entitled "Lay it right on top of us!" The article read: "For a decision he made in a Vietnam battle—to call an air strike on himself and his men of Charlie Company—Captain William Carpenter has been recommended for the Medal of Honor." (In reality, Carpenter earned his second Silver Star for this action, an award soon upgraded to the Distinguished Service Cross. He retired as a lieutenant general.)

The article went on to state some soldiers had suffered burns, but that the strike gave Charlie Company the breather it desperately needed:

"Right after that napalm," said Carpenter, "enemy fire stopped completely for maybe twenty minutes." His first sergeant added, "Those twenty minutes gave us the thing we most needed: time to reorganize and build up a perimeter."

Scant mention was made of the United States Air Force F-4s that dropped the napalm.

What a breathtaking account! I gradually learned some war events were reported as propaganda to make the Johnson Administration look good. This article was factual, written by a well-regarded *Life* correspondent. I was vicariously being drawn into the politics of the war and felt a duty to preserve pertinent articles about Vietnam as well as op-eds and photographs. Most civilians I knew from my former life weren't interested in my world. We military wives were anomalies. I'm glad I stayed at MacDill for the duration, rather than return to Saint Louis or Chicago.

Many articles and TV specials appeared in the years after Vietnam. Not until thirty years later did I realize the ramifications of Johnson's unforgivable duplicity. It reared its ugly face in 2003 when his Secretary of Defense, Robert McNamara, was interviewed for the film, *The Fog of War*. He admitted that the reason for going to war in 1964—a supposed unprovoked aggressive act in the Gulf of Tonkin—was a pretext based on incomplete, misleading information.

Here's what happened, according to a project called *Vietnam: The Art of War*, which presents the interpretations of Vietnamese journalists and artists: Two of our destroyers—the USS *Maddox* and USS *Turner Joy*—were in the Gulf of Tonkin. On August 2, 1964, the *Maddox* fired upon three North Vietnamese patrol boats poised to attack. The *Maddox*, along with navy fighter jets, fended off the boats. Two were heavily damaged and retreated. The other was destroyed. Two days later, the *Turner Joy* joined its sister ship. Under poor visibility they maneuvered to avoid any more attacks though it was unclear whether any North Vietnamese boats were actually in pursuit.

The Art of War website quotes Squadron Commander James Stockdale, who was flying reconnaissance over the Gulf of Tonkin. "I had the best seat in the house to watch that event and our destroyers were just shooting at phantom targets," he reported later. "There were no PT boats there...there was nothing there but black water and American firepower."

In his book *Presidents of War*, Michael Beschloss writes that President Johnson privately told Under Secretary of State George Ball, "Hell, those dumb, stupid sailors were just shooting at flying fish." Johnson and McNamara pressed Congress to pass the Gulf of Tonkin Resolution, a legal authorization for war. Soon after the resolution had passed, the Pentagon and U.S. intelligence secretly informed both men there had been no second attack on August 4. Yet Johnson did not inform Congress and the public that his information had been faulty. Beschloss concludes that Johnson used the Gulf of Tonkin Resolution as his warrant to prosecute the war. He even carried the resolution in his wallet during the rest of his presidency.

Bernie wrote back in the fall of 1965, shortly after the squadron arrived at Cam Ranh, that his commander in chief personally picked their bombing targets—a dangerous and futile exercise that brought little success. Bombing the Ho Chi Minh Trail, the enemy's supply route, was one example. Though the Viet Cong repaired the damage in record time, the strikes continued. Yet crucial targets, such as the missile sites in Hanoi, were off-limits for fear of escalating the war and provoking North Vietnam's allies, Communist China and the Soviet Union. This made me angry. What was the point? It all seemed so political, so futile.

My cousin, Mark Berent, an F-4 fighter pilot who served four tours in Vietnam from 1965 to 1973, spoke scathingly of the so-called "rules of engagement" that restricted our military forces to a no-win strategy.

"We were forced to fight the war with one hand tied behind our back, one eye blinded, and only half a pocket full of ammunition," he told me.

Mark rued the loss of airmen because of rules forbidding pre-emptive targets. Eighty percent of POWs (prisoners of war) were aircrew members. Many were shot down by surface-to-air missile (SAM) sites they watched being built but weren't allowed to destroy.

It took years for the truth to trickle out. By 2018, when *Presidents of War* was published, I was more saddened than surprised to learn what LBJ said to his advisers in 1965, the year Bernie was sent to Cam Ranh Bay: "I don't think anything is going to be as bad as losing, and I don't see any way of winning."

In the mid-1960s I realized I was living through an historical era. It was a shameful time that brought protests and anti-military sentiments. It was a time when the general public forgot American prisoners of war. Thankfully, their courageous family members lobbied to free them and a few conscientious politicians listened.

The 1972 photo of Hollywood actress Jane Fonda sitting on a North Vietnamese anti-aircraft gun emplacement in North Vietnam appalled me.

During her visit to Hanoi, she also made several radio announcements over Voice of Vietnam radio imploring US pilots to stop the bombings. After her visit she earned the nickname "Hanoi Jane," according to a 2018 *Washington Post* retrospective about her trip. At the time some lawmakers called her actions treason. The Veterans of Foreign Wars passed a resolution calling for her to be prosecuted as a traitor. Congress held hearings.

Fonda married the anti-war activist, Tom Hayden. In his memoir, *Reunion*, he recounts reporters asking him to comment on the Paris Peace Accords, signed in January of 1973. He writes: "I recall snapping back that the POWs were liars, hypocrites, and pawns in Nixon's efforts to rewrite history. Jane remembers that it was actually she who made the comment."

Years later, the actress admitted her regrets about her Hanoi trip, but the damage had been done. To many, she will always be America's wartime traitor. Many veterans and others would not forgive her. I joined them in their condemnation.

When Johnson announced he would not run for reelection in March 1968, Bernie and I were overjoyed. Our gazes met in a hallelujah moment. The words would come later, after the war ended in April 1975 and some of the machinations behind it seeped into the light.

The war ended long ago, but the animosity toward our soldiers who fought there took longer to fade away. It did, though, especially after the Gulf War.

When Bernie and I visited the Vietnam Veterans Memorial in Washington, DC, we touched the names of his squadron mates. I made rubbings of their names. The last person whose name I preserved was Denny Eilers, Bernie's fraternity brother and college roommate. All the words written about the war melted into tears as we stood before the 58,286 names solemnly displayed. Framed photos, letters, medals, and other mementos of loss sat on the ground beneath the long, long lists.

Flowers didn't say enough.

Chapter 10

HOME AT LAST

Lisa welcomes Daddy home!

I often imagined how romantic Bernie's homecoming would be. Would we wives be waiting in the hangar as the plane rolled up? Would Richard Rodgers's theme ring in my ears as it did in *Victory at Sea*, when the ship pulls in and all those sailors clamber down the gangplank to their wives' loving arms?

One hot September day, two months before Bernie's homecoming, I was hanging Paul's diapers on the backyard clothesline. No luscious palm trees dotted our back yard. There were no trees at all. I'd get one line filled up and the diapers would be dry before

I started the next row. Paul was in his playpen in the Florida room with Lisa. I saw them through the window.

The kitchen phone rang. I dropped my basket and dashed inside.

"Hello. Is this Mrs. Bernard Giere?

"Yes."

"This is the Red Cross calling."

"Oh?"

"We have some news of your husband."

"Yes? News? Why?"

"Lieutenant Giere is all right. He was shot down over North Vietnam but was rescued by helicopter and has not been injured." I grabbed a chair and sat down. "He'll be coming home soon."

"When?"

"You will be informed shortly."

"Thank you," I said, and hung up.

My eyes turned to the family room. Lisa was hanging Bernie's handkerchiefs over a clothesline I had rigged for her. Paul seemed content to watch from his playpen and listen to her running commentary. Ordinarily I'd sop up this scene to remember for Bernie, but my focus was on my pulsing heartbeats. *Take hold, Sarajane. Carry on.* I walked out the door to get the laundry basket. *What am I doing? What in the hell did she say? Bernie was shot down? What about BerJim? Oh, shit. I can't even remember.*

I went back into the house, took out paper and pen, and called the Red Cross. Yes, I had heard correctly. I was to call the squadron commander's wife to get details, which were being forwarded to MacDill headquarters right now. I talked to Sandi. She'd also gotten a call. Jim was fine. We later learned that, upon their return to CRB, the colonel called in both Jim and Bernie and announced he was sending them home early.

Jim and Bernie told the story of their rescue many times, Jim in a written first-person account, Bernie in speeches and interviews:

On September 16, 1966, Jim and Bernie flew the last aircraft in a flight of three F-4s tasked with bombing a target before the weather turned bad. They had to fly beneath a three thousand-foot cloud cover to get to the target in the southern part of North Vietnam, approximately eighty miles into the demilitarized zone (DMZ). Because of ground fire the approach procedure for F-4 missions was to "make one pass and haul ass." Staying under an overcast at 2,800 feet, they rolled in and felt a loud, hard explosion on the bottom of the airplane. Flack is designed to explode and send out shrapnel to damage/destroy aircraft, but in their case, they got a direct hit on the way up to reach altitude. Bernie learned later there were eighty-five anti-aircraft guns around the target.

"The first plane to fly over woke them up, "Bernie said. "The second one got them mad, and they started shooting at number three."

"Our F-4 jumped straight up, like the 'kick in the butt' you get when you light the afterburners," Jim remembered, "except this time that sensation was vertical and not forward."

Bernie rolled the plane out of its planned course and pulled it straight up through the clouds. At three thousand feet he jettisoned all the external equipment and weapons. Both engines were running, with a fire light on one and an overheat light on the other. They transmitted that they were hit and headed east-southeast toward the ocean and/or the DMZ. They hoped to limp to sea for a pickup but that idea was quickly scrubbed when the F-4's right engine seized and the left caught on fire. Then they lost the hydraulics and nosed over sharply at ten thousand feet, going into a violent dive. Without hydraulics, the F-4 is uncontrollable.

"Bailout, bailout, bailout!" Bernie yelled, but Jim was forced up against the canopy.

"I can't!" he yelled back. "Negative Gs!" He was struggling to reach the D-ring between his knees. He kept at it and at it.

99

"I distinctly remember thinking I was dead," Jim wrote.

The pilot up front needs to wait for the Guy in the Back Seat (GIB) to eject first. If the front-seater goes first, the rockets that blast his ejection seat out of the plane will burn the pilot sitting behind. However, when an airplane at low altitude spins in an uncontrolled dive, survival is measured in milliseconds.

"I don't know at what point Ben was going to stop waiting for me and get out himself," Jim recalled, "but it should have been long ago. Finally, I felt something with my fingertips and, bending as hard as I could, I reached and pulled the ejection handle."

An F-4 pilot wears a large parachute and harness that buckles into his seat. When he pulls the levers under his legs, rocket charges fire to blow the aircraft canopy away and then rocket boosters under his "ass" take the whole seat, with him in it, up and out of the jet. Within seconds he should be floating over the falling aircraft with a parachute canopy fluttering over his head.

Bernie's ejection ripped a hole in his chute. He hit hard upon landing, but his two-way radio, part of his survival gear, remained intact. The burning wreckage and the two pilots formed a fifty-yard triangle on the ground. That was the last Bernie and Jim saw each other until they were rescued. Both were in twenty-foot "elephant" grass, and they were not the only ones there.

My pilot recalled, "I heard the bad guys calling to each other on bullhorns, trying to find us. All I could think about was, *Shit! Looks like it's fish heads and rice for dinner tonight.* His chute was caught in the tall grass, a dead giveaway to his trail all the way back to his parachute.

Bernie talked to the other two F-4s circling overhead, who told him they could stay for twenty minutes for close air support and that a Jolly Green Giant was on the way.

Jim described going through the field of grass: "The farther I got, the thicker it got, and I was soon crawling on my hands and knees. Every time I stopped, I could hear the search party so I kept going deeper. I honestly couldn't see more than six or so inches in front of me."

A few minutes later, both of them heard the distinct sounds of a helicopter approaching. Jim was first to spot it and homed them in on his location.

The rescuers came directly over Jim and dropped a jungle penetrator—a heavy, metallic, bullet-shaped device on a cable that's designed to go into dense vegetation. Its arms were folded up during the drop but folded down during pickup, allowing him to put his legs over them and be hoisted out. Jim jumped on it and was hauled up.

When Bernie saw them fly away, he yelled into his radio.

"Hey guys, come back, come back. There's another one down here!"

Jim always teased him about that. The wait must have seemed like hours, but it was only a few minutes before the HH-3E helicopter, known as the Jolly Green Giant, circled back and rescued Bernie. Both passengers were okay.

Captain David E. Dickey commanded that helicopter rescue crew, out of a marine combat base on the southern edge of the DMZ at Dong Ha. On board were First Lieutenant John E. Halligan, copilot; Tech Sergeant Fred C. Williams, mechanic; and Airman Second Class Robert F. Gabourel, rescue specialist. Its crew had been monitoring the guys' strike frequency. When

Bernie giving the dedication speech for the restoration of the HH-3E Helicopter, 2008.

they heard Bernie say they'd been hit, they jumped into their Jolly Green and headed right for them.

Upon arrival at the chopper's base, Bernie called their command post at Cam Ranh Bay to check in. When he came back, he looked at Jimmy and grinned.

"Well," Jimmy asked, "what did the colonel say?"

"Colonel Chase told me that since it was my second ejection and your third, they decided we didn't have to fly any more combat and could go home."

"What did you say?

"I said, 'Yes, sir. That's what we called to tell you.'"

Jim and the other squadron pilots always chuckled about Bernie's answer, even though nobody really knew if he was telling the truth. To joke about it was most likely the relief they needed at the time.

That telephone conversation stuck for the next fifty years. Much later my pilot told me that the colonel said they'd lost enough planes already and couldn't afford to lose any more!

One sentence from Jim's firsthand account jumped out at me: "I don't know at what point Ben was going to stop waiting for me and get out himself, but it should have been long ago." Their lifelong bond was so easy to understand. Jim's life depended on Bernie, who waited a few extra seconds for his GIB to make it out. I know if their places had been switched, Jim would have done the same for Bernie.

Told and retold, often humorously, the rescue story became part of their psyches, their compact for life. As Jim wrote, "Ben Giere and I shared an almost identical airline career and nearly shared a grave. It's hard to imagine a closer bond than that."

Their near-death experience, rendered in their own words, gives the incident an immediacy that lives on and shows me the meaning of courage and love. As was written in John 13:15,

"Greater love than this no man hath, that a man lay down his life for his friends." (Douay-Rheims 1899 American Edition)

A representative from the Martin-Baker Aircraft Company, a British company that made the ejection seats, told Jim his three ejections tied him with a navy guy for the record. The representative also said it was impossible to do what Jim did without breaking his back.

After that, Bernie and Jim became members of the exclusive Martin-Baker Ejection Tie Club, which unifies all pilots whose lives the company had helped save. The ties are blue silk with an M-B emblem. Martin-Baker supplies ejection seats for ninety-three air forces worldwide. In 2016 the company claimed the seats have saved 7,545 lives since the first live ejection test in 1946. I still have Bernie's tie.

The following is excerpted from a Mission Narrative Report made by the rescue officer on September 18, 1966:

> With favorable help from Bird Dog (the planes circling overhead) the first crew member was found and rescued within 18 minutes. Although the other crew member was only 50 yards away, some trouble was experienced in finding him because of excessive radio chatter and dense under bush. Again, Bird Dog guided Jolly Green 15 to the second crew member and he too was removed from hostile environment. Total elapsed time for both pickups was 20 minutes. I returned to Dong Ha to off-load the two crew members who were met by an air force vehicle. Total elapsed mission time was 30 minutes.
>
> All support aircraft did a fine job. No aircraft were used against enemy positions. No enemy ground fire was encountered during the aircrew recovery. Both pilots were in good physical condition except for minor scratches about the head. Both downed pilots remained calm and composed during the entire pick up which was accomplished by hoist and jungle penetrator.

To the officer who filed the report, it was one successful rescue drama among many, but to Sandi and me, this rescue was the Fourth of July! First Lieutenant Bernard D. Giere had just completed his 214th, and last, mission with 433:25 combat hours in the F-4C. During that time seven pilots in his squadron had died. One had been sent home with injuries, another when his wife died, a third when his son died of crib death.

John Flanagan, a forward air controller whom Bernie met through the air national guard and author of *Vietnam Above the Treetops*, wrote of Bernie's last flight: "The commander thought it better that they go home before their year was up. Bernie was jump-qualified, a graduate of the army's rigorous parachute training course. He surmised that the 'paranoid powers' thought he was earning his senior parachutist badge at the expense of the air force's F-4s."

Lisa and Paul welcoming Daddy home!

I had only a few hours warning for Bernie's homecoming. After the call came I stayed up late, washed my hair, gave the place the once-over, nursed Paul, wandered the house, tried to read, fed Paul again, and finally fell into bed. The next morning when Bernie arrived by cab, we three were waiting. Our Santa walked in with duffel bag in tow and a suitcase full of presents.

Santa's face lit up as he dropped his bags, surveyed the scene, and kissed us, one by one. Lisa tugged at her daddy's pant leg and led him to the sofa. Four-month-old Paul squirmed in his infant seat, feet pumping away, a look of wonder on his chubby little face.

Bernie sat down. Lisa plopped into his lap. She fingered his hair and patted his cheeks, checked out his tie, and then hugged him with all the power of a three-year-old, as if to say, *He's mine!* I held back and let her take over, knowing my turn would come in the fullness of time.

Having Bernie home was a seamless transition, as if we'd always been a family of four. We savored each minute together. Life seemed to appear in small dramas before me as I watched Bernie play with Lisa or feed the baby or take us to the park. We rented a motel room near where he'd had a few days of firing range practice in Avon Park, Florida. The motel owners' daughter watched the kids while we ate out at a French restaurant they had recommended—a luxurious villa in the middle of nowhere. Florida did have its perks, after all.

The romance of our togetherness during that post-war year stayed with me. I could call it up at will. Watching Bernie with the kids was a joyful scene I never forgot.

Each night after dinner, we sat on the front porch, Paul next to us in his infant seat, and watched Lisa ride her tricycle in front of the house. Vietnam wasn't a topic of conversation. Instead we discussed Bernie's upcoming job as an instructor at MacDill—a position that would last a year until his obligation was completed. His parents were looking forward to our visit soon and to the baptism we'd have for Paul in their neighborhood church where Bernie had been baptized. Those evening front porch planning sessions were the tonic we needed, I thought, to settle us back to a normal life again. A normal life? Was I going to be surprised.

While peddling her trike down our driveway, Lisa spotted a small silvery paper on the grass and brought it over.

"Looks interesting," Bernie said, tucking it into his pocket.

After Mr. X left his house the next day, I ventured near their carport and found more rolling papers for pot in the grass. Soon after I spied Mr. X from my utility room window as he took the seats out of his car and hosed down the interior. Bernie called Detective Flynn.

"Yes, this is significant evidence," he said. "Sounds like drugs."

Flynn met Bernie at a 7-Eleven and took the evidence. A few months later, he called us to say they had the conviction they needed to finally send Mr. X up for life.

"You should be proud of yourself, Sherlock," Bernie said, shaking my hand.

I was. For both of us.

Our first night out after Vietnam.

PART 3

"Love is the discovery of ourselves in others and the delight in the recognition."

— Alexander McCall Smith

Chapter 11

IOWA

Crossroads appeared suddenly like gradient pointers stretching miles and miles, eventually lost in a Grant Wood landscape. This was the Iowa I loved. Seeing it again after four years would change me.

Whiffs from farm brush fires drifted in the car vent as we glided along Route 30. This was the first time we'd been alone together since Bernie had returned from Vietnam a month earlier. Our kids were with his parents in Chicago.

"This will be my last mission," Bernie said. His fraternity brother Denny Eilers was missing in action. We were on our way to visit his wife, Belva. I suggested we drive by our first apartment before going to the Eilers' Tipton farm.

Cedar Rapids seemed welcoming, at first even romantic. Our honeymoon attic apartment windows looked out to a fire escape and down Second Avenue, a street guarded by a regiment of elm trees that dusted away the drabness and make the neighborhood look classy. That first winter, the radiators hissed and pinged and generated enough heat to keep us lovebirds bedded down in our nest, as the outside temperature hovered around zero.

The campus trees were aflame in fall colors. We smelled the aromas from the Quaker Oats factory furnaces across the Cedar

River. Life in our old college town seemed unchanged, like a *tableau vivant*. But all I could think about was how different we were. A brutal war was being fought eight thousand miles away, and who cared except us?

We headed for the outskirts of town.

When Bernie said, "You can always tell a place has good food by the number of trucks parked out front," I knew we were headed for the Pine Inn, a fraternity favorite.

"What kind of man would take my daughter to a truck stop for dinner?" my mother had asked when we dated.

"Trust me, Mother," I'd said. "He's German. It's not the atmosphere. It's the food that counts."

I floated into the restaurant and breathed in that familiar pine scent. The daily specials were scrawled on the chalkboard, as they always were.

"What'll ya' have?" the waitress asked as she plunked down the metal-tipped menus. Bernie didn't miss a beat.

"We'll have two beers, one pork tenderloin sandwich special, with all the trimmings, and the lady will have just the tenderloin."

"Got it."

Bernie was the thinnest I'd ever seen him. I was glad he was piling it on.

We talked about the time we and the Eilers drove to Carlsbad Caverns in New Mexico when Denny and Bernie were both at pilot training bases in West Texas.

"Remember those bats flying out of the caves by the thousands?" I asked.

"I only remember hitting the deer as we left," Bernie said. "How you and Belva screeched and howled at poor Bambi."

"We did *not*. We were just upset when that man in the pickup truck behind us slit the doe's throat and pulled her over to the side of the road. You and Denny got out and watched it all. 'It's food for the orphanage,' the guy told you."

110

"I think he was from Colorado," Bernie said. "He had quite a knife."

My pilot worked his way through his beer and ordered another.

"Denny's plane was an old AC-47, a cargo plane converted into a lethal gunship with a crew of six. The Viet Cong called it the Dragon in the Sky, but we called it Spooky, or Puff the Magic Dragon." This was the most Bernie had talked about the war. I wanted to hear more. Yet I didn't want to probe too deeply. He had written me about his seven squadron mates who'd died, and now Denny was missing.

Four men were having a noisy meal at the next table. Dressed in plaid flannel shirts, boots, overalls, and jeans, they were straight out of a Thomas Hart Benton mural of rural America. I wondered if they knew or cared about what was happening in Southeast Asia.

Bernie lowered his voice.

"Denny's missions were top secret," he explained. "They were flying low-level strafing missions, supporting the special forces camps in Laos. Shit! You're not even supposed to know we're *flying* in Laos. I flew missions there, too, along the Ho Chi Min Trail."

I was working up a noticeable heartbeat. I recalled when Bernie first wrote me about flying the trail. He said I should burn the letters, but I never did. My optimism about the war's outcome was crumbling.

"Denny could be in the Hanoi Hilton, couldn't he?" I asked. "I heard some POWs might have been taken to Russia or China."

Bernie spun his lighter around on the place mat and pulled out a cigarette.

"It's possible, but not likely."

I focused on Belva. *What am I going to say to her?*

Bernie and I left the restaurant and paused outside the entrance. I put my arms around him, not wanting to move an inch. He smiled and pulled me closer, then kissed me.

We rode silently, in tune with the rhythm of the road, around gentle curves, over rolling hills. Iowa was the antidote for the heat and humidity of Tampa. The seasons changed; the harvests marked time with a multitude of colors on the palette.

Belva and the boys.

Belva and the boys were standing on the front porch when we arrived. Upon seeing them, a rush of sadness welled up. I suppressed it as they came down to greet us.

"Captain Giere is Daddy's friend," Belva said, hugging Bernie. "And this is Sarajane, his wife. Say hello, boys."

"Hello," said the oldest, the picture of Denny. His little brother clutched his Tonka Tractor, his eyes on the pilot.

"Bernie and your daddy were fraternity brothers at Coe," she said, and then to me, softly, "It seems like ages ago, doesn't it?"

I smiled. Words deserted me. The boys stared.

Belva brought out coffee and cookies. The room bespoke elegance. The green damask drapes echoed the pattern colors in the

Oriental carpet. The boys were on their knees, running their Match-box cars over the designs. I wondered what was coming next.

When the kids took their cars into the dining room, Belva perched expectantly on the edge of the sofa.

"I ran into Denny on the flight line at Ton San Nhut last December," Bernie said. "We wanted to get together after that, somehow. He looked good, enthusiastic about the missions."

"I know they were dangerous," Belva said. "If anyone could take care of himself, Denny could. Couldn't he?"

Bernie nodded.

"I must have been in shock when I found out," she said. "I still can't believe it, but I'm hopeful he's still alive."

She glanced at me, then to Bernie, who cleared his throat and emptied his coffee cup.

"You're right, there's still hope. Just keep the communications open with the state department. Don't let the red tape get you down."

When we rose to leave it was dark. We said goodbye to the boys and I followed Bernie and Belva to the car, thanking God with every step that my pilot had come back. Belva hugged us both.

"Please keep in touch, you two," she said.

As we pulled onto the highway, I turned to glance at Bernie's somber profile.

"How long will she have to wait to find out anything?" I asked.

"It could be a long time, I'm afraid. We're not supposed to be in Laos, and that makes the search almost impossible, for now."

"What do you think will happen?" I asked.

"My opinion is, he didn't make it. No facts yet, just my gut feeling."

"You mean you think he's dead?" My eyes filled up, ready to pour.

"I'm sorry, hon, but I couldn't dash her hopes. I couldn't be the one. What if I were wrong? What if he *is* a POW?"

"Oh, my God. Why didn't you tell me this before?"

Bernie tried to pull me closer to him, but I resisted.

"You should have told me." The gusher flowed freely. I felt blood rising to my cheeks as I scooted nearer the window. "How can you be so certain?"

"That AC-47 was a death trap. His flight leader's plane had also been shot down that day."

"Oh, no. All those men."

"If they don't discover the crew within seven years—maybe more, considering it was in Laos—they could be declared KIA (killed in action). Then maybe she'll be able to get on with her life."

I cupped my hands over my face. My pilot was so horribly matter-of-fact, so blatant.

"I can't believe you're saying this." I rested my head against the window and sighed. Bernie pulled out his handkerchief and passed it to me. My year of persistent longing had ended, but Belva's was just beginning.

The lonely farms sat shrouded in darkness as I said a silent goodbye to Iowa and who I was when we lived there. Was it only five years ago that we were college kids? Campus traditions like homecoming had taken on a frantic importance then. Bernie had turned an old car into a submarine for the Tau Kappa Epsilon's homecoming parade float. I went to watch the guys build it. I cheered as Bernie popped his head out of the conning tower when it rolled by. The crowds loved it. So did I.

The next year we settled down as honeymooners, trying on our roles as husband and wife three stories above Second Avenue. On the wall of our sparsely furnished living room hung two of my paintings from Marvin Cone's art class at Coe. We thought they made the room look rich and refined. Cone, my wonderful art teacher, introduced me to oil painting my freshman year and gifted me with a lifelong love of the art.

Bernie thought our creaky little apartment was perfect. When he was away, however, it wasn't so hospitable. I never told him that the first night I slept there alone, I had a baseball bat under my bed. He'd been chosen to attend a weekend encampment for campus leaders and there I was, shivering, as the leaves danced against the windowpane. Someone knocked on our downstairs door. I grabbed my bat, sat up in bed, and pretended no one was home.

When we sped past the Pine Inn, I turned away from the window, away from the newlyweds, Bernie and Sarajane. I knew I'd never be the same again. I survived Bernie's year in Vietnam, and, if I had to, I could do it again.

After Denny's plane was shot down in 1965, the crew was listed as MIA (missing in action). Denny and all crew members weren't declared dead until 1977. During those years, the men were promoted several times. Denny went from captain to lieutenant colonel. The war ended on April 30, 1975, when the North Vietnamese rolled through the gates of the Presidential Palace in Saigon, South Vietnam.

In 1995 the Laos People's Democratic Republic finally let a search team investigate the site where Denny's plane probably had crashed. Follow-up investigations were made in 1999 and 2001. The site was excavated five times between then and July 2011.

One day in 2012, while Bernard was reading the Long Island paper, *Newsday*, he became excited at an article about a local airman whose remains were being returned from Vietnam.

"From the description, he must have been part of Denny's crew," Bernie said, softly.

My dear husband was finding it hard to control his emotions. We both teared up. My tears came more for him than Denny. He couldn't call Belva, and neither could I, for fear of losing control.

In April 2012, more than forty-six years after Denny's plane went down, the air force notified survivors that in addition to a tooth fragment positively identified as belonging to a crew member, approximately one hundred bone fragments had been labeled as "group remains" of the six-man crew.

Denny Eilers and the other men were honored on July 9, 2012 when they were laid to rest at Arlington National Cemetery. A horse-drawn caisson bearing a single casket took them to their final resting place. A single white marker, including the names of all six men, was placed on the common gravesite.

Eventually, Belva had married Duffy Schamberger, Bernie's fraternity brother, a widower with three children. I saw Belva at a Coe reunion and we spoke about those early days. Duffy was a great husband and father, she said, and that didn't surprise me.

Walking across campus brought back an earlier version of myself. In spite of a few high-rise buildings and the disappearance of Old Main, which had held Marvin Cone's art studios on the third floor, the campus looked the same.

On the ride back to Chicago, with thoughts of Coe on my mind, I realized my most valuable education really began when I left Iowa in 1962 and moved to Texas to become an air force wife.

Chapter 12

HELLO, PAN AM

We ushered in 1967, knowing that by October, Bernie would be wearing civvies. It seemed too good to be true. He was fulfilling his last year in the United States Air Force as a MacDill flight instructor, a duty that gave us time to be a family again and Bernie time to search for the perfect airline job. A captain, he was making a decent salary of $928 a month. He duly noted the sum in his spiral-bound record book as carefully as if he were recording his flight time, which was golden in the aviation world.

Civilian? Hell, yes! Squadron pilots at the time felt that if they made the air force a career, another war assignment would be forthcoming.

The airlines looked like a good bet. My sister Germaine, a former stewardess, had written Bernie at Cam Ranh that Pan Am and TWA were buying the 747 "Jumbo Jets," Boeing's pride. These two international carriers needed pilots badly, especially men with air force experience. What better incentive did Bernie need?

My worries about stranger-than-fiction neighbors were put to rest after Mr. X and the Jacksons were gone. Porch sitting after dinner became a delight. Bernie was happy with his job at MacDill and the prospects before him, feeling lucky to have interviews with five airline carriers. We plotted the future, revisiting our options each night.

TWA called him back to take another electrocardiogram because they'd detected a heart murmur in the first one. This gave us pause. I remembered Bernie telling me about a heart murmur he'd had in 1956.

When Bernie was seven, his three-year-old younger brother, Carlie, died of a congenital heart defect called Blue Baby Syndrome, or cyanotic heart disease. Carlie's skin had a bluish tint, Bernie recalled, especially on his lips and fingers. I'd never heard his parents speak of Carlie until Christmas 1964 when Lisa and I stayed with Rudy and Gretel while Bernie was on temporary assignment in Okinawa.

One Sunday afternoon, on the way back from lunch at Howard Johnson's, Bernie's parents said they wanted to stop at Eden Memorial Park to see Carlie's grave. I hadn't planned on this. When I recall that afternoon, with Lisa and me in the back seat, I realize I talked too much. I asked Rudy and Gretel questions about the successful open-heart surgeries that had begun on blue babies in 1944. Rudy raised his arm to brush back a tear. I was stepping onto delicate ground. My spirits sank. Even after eighteen years, the pain of losing such a beautiful, curly-haired little boy was great. I sat back and turned to Lisa for gentle relief.

I thought of Winston Churchill, who had also lost a child around the tender age of three. The joyful little girl's name was Marigold. Her father had nicknamed her "Duckadilly." Winston and Clementine found it hard to dismiss their grief, too, according to William Manchester's *The Last Lion: William Spencer Churchill, Visions of Glory, 1874-1932.* Seven months after Marigold's death, Winston wrote to his wife, "Poor lamb—it is a gaping wound, whenever one touches it and removes the bandages and plasters of daily life."

Years later, when recalling Rudy's uncharacteristic reaction, I realized his son's death must have been the most poignant chapter in their marriage—one that led to Gretel's depression as Bernie grew up. Rudy dealt with this loss in his own way, accepting succor from their church family and supporting Gretel through her darkest days with comfort and love. From then on, the compassion I felt for my in-laws supplanted any complaints I had about their unwavering living habits.

Bernie flew back to TWA headquarters in Kansas City and took another EKG, which was normal. I breathed easily after that and tried to erase any negative notions I harbored, just as I'd tried to do but couldn't quite manage when Bernie was bailing out of airplanes in Vietnam. I thanked God my pilot passed the test this time. Yet I wondered what we would've done if he'd been denied an airline job because of a questionable EKG. I also knew the airlines required their pilots to pass medical exams annually. What would happen if the anomaly showed up again?

One evening Lisa begged to see the new boy who had just moved in down the street.

"Okay," Bernie said. "Invite him over."

"Lisa says he's from New York," I told Bernie as the two kids escorted each other to our front yard.

"This is Joey," Lisa said. "He's from Brooklyn. He talks funny."

Joey smiled proudly. A dead ringer for a six-year-old Mickey Rooney, Joey seemed a friendly boy. He was a nonstop talker. After they ran to his house to play, I turned to Bernie.

"Well, dear," I said, "looks like we have normal neighbors at last."

"About time," he said, smiling.

Bernie sanctioned the friendship after he met Joey's dad, who said he was a salesman. For a few months, all went well. Three-year-old Lisa was busy with her new friend, and Bernie was busy with his instructor job while arranging his airline physicals and interviews.

Wally, Bernie's pal from the 555th, had left the service the year before and called Bernie to tell him how he loved being with Pan Am. He was a navigator and soon-to-be flight engineer. He encouraged Bernie to apply.

"After training, you can name where you'd rather be stationed, San Francisco or New York," he said. Bernie admitted this setup sounded ideal, but he also wondered if he could pass muster for what was then called the "world's most experienced" airline.

Bernie sitting on an engine intake.

Started in 1927, the airline was the largest international air carrier in the US. It held a lofty position in the popular culture of the Cold War era. In November 1935 Pan Am commissioned the Glenn L. Martin Company to build the China Clipper, the first of three Martin M-130 four-engine flying boats. Thus began the airline's flying legacy of travel called "The Lindbergh Trail," so named because Charles Lindbergh sat on the company's board of directors starting right after World War II.

A Pan Am plane forms the backdrop for some famous images, including the 1964 arrival of the Beatles at JFK aboard the Boeing 707-321 Clipper, Defiance. Following that, Pan Am 707s were in airport scenes in James Bond movies.

In the end my pilot was accepted by all five airlines he applied to. He decided on Pan American World Airways out of JFK. He would start as a flight engineer, earning between $1,400 and $1,700 dollars a month, which he felt was fine for an entry-level job.

Jim, Bernie's cockpit mate at Cam Ranh, also chose Pan Am. When Jim's wife, Sandi, and I heard that we'd all be moving to New York in October, we couldn't believe our good fortune.

On one of those late summer, sultry nights, as Bernie puttered in the front yard, Lisa came back from Joey's, excited about watching cartoons in their garage. Bernie had mentioned the stockpiles of movies he saw there when he went over to meet Joey's dad.

"The grown-ups watch movies, too," Lisa said, "but we're not allowed to see them."

Bernie grew curious. Something was amiss. I could sense it. If Joey's dad were just showing movies, why did he have such stockpiles of them? Was he selling them? If so, they couldn't have been reruns of the *Andy Griffith Show*.

"What do you think?" I asked Bernie. "Are they in the dirty movie business?"

"Well, let's not get hasty," he replied. "What proof do we have? You know how Lisa exaggerates." Bernie took his time making decisions. He was waffling. I reminded him that even though his daughter could be a dramatist at times, she could understand remarks uttered by perfect strangers to see if they were genuine human beings.

"And that's not the meat of it," I continued. "Don't you remember? Mr. X moved in next door to appear like a normal person. Our neighborhood gave him a cover of respectability so he could fly to Miami and pull off his heists."

We wondered how much Joey knew about this movie business. Rather than question the "little operator," as Bernie dubbed him, the pilot surprised me when he contacted our favorite detective, Sergeant Flynn.

"No kidding," Flynn said. "I'll look into it." I was relieved.

This detective business was old hat at that point. We left it to our sergeant to take over. The future was what held us captive—Pan Am, selling our house, and moving to New York. We cared less about what was going on two doors down in the garage piled high with movie canisters. Lisa was busy at nursery school. Even though I couldn't prove anything untoward was taking place at Joey's, I didn't let her wander too far from home without my approval.

We found a realtor and put our house on the market, assuring him we had terrific neighbors and thinking the place would go in a week or two. Such a great little neighborhood!

Then Sergeant Flynn called: Joey's dad was a known figure in the pornography world of Brooklyn. Experienced as we were with nefarious Tampa neighbors, I couldn't help but ask Bernie, "Why us?" He gave me a wink of an answer.

"We're just lucky, I guess," he said.

Within the month Joey and his mom moved back to New York while the hardware salesman faced charges.

Bernie left for Pan Am training in New York and rented an apartment on Long Beach with Jim. My sister was waiting to host us at her home in Stony Brook, Long Island, until we found a place of our own.

While I searched for a house, Bernie worked his way through training as a flight engineer on a 7O7, Boeing's first commercial jet, a midsize, long-range, four-engine passenger aircraft. Built between 1957 and 1979, it was the first jet airliner to carry passengers for long distances.

I'd never heard of a flight engineer.

"A flight engineer is a member of the aircraft's flight crew who monitors and operates its complex aircraft systems, such as the electrical, pneumatic, fuel, and hydraulic systems," Bernie said. Then he smiled. I knew a punch line was coming. "You might say, my dear, I'm a special operator."

"You sure are," I said.

He went on to explain that flight engineers usually stayed in that position their entire career. By the late '60s, with so many ex-military pilots applying to the airlines, the position was a necessary stepping-stone to first officer (copilot), then captain. The older career engineers, formally called air mechanics, were not qualified to pilot the plane. Most young navigators and engineers, such as Bernie, could.

My pilot was happy. His contentment became mine, too, making me even more eager to sell our house and join him in New York. I was itching to leave Tampa behind and move on to my sister's place. Finally, after six weeks, we got an offer we liked. The sale went through.

Never had I thought of living on a Long Island farm, but that's what we did in October 1967. I found a house on a big potato farm in Saint James, New York, five minutes from my sister's place in Stony Brook and less than an hour's drive to JFK airport. I visualized us living there the minute I saw the place and signed the rental agreement without hesitation. I knew Bernie would approve.

The cozy, red ranch on the Hartman Farm sat on Moriches Road with potato fields behind it and across the road. Saint James's main street showcased a typical small town lifted from some long-ago scrapbook. The impeccable modest homes, a century-old general store, and quaint shops along the main thoroughfare excited me. It was a welcome world away from Tampa. Located on Long Island's North Shore near Long Island Sound, it had its own train station, which meant I heard trains coming and going. They were music to my ears.

A few years later, I learned two intriguing things about the town. The first was delivered matter-of-factly to me by a mom I met at the elementary school down the street. I'd just told her about Tampa's Mr. X.

"I'm glad you're not uncomfortable among gangsters," she said, laughing, "because Saint James is home to a reputed mobster."

After I informed Bernie about the mafioso, he said drolly, "Hey kid, I told you we're moving up in the world!"

I found the second treasure of trivia hidden in Saint James one sunny October morning. Lisa was in second grade. Paul was helping his dad pick potato bugs off the tomato plants in our garden. I sailed along Lake Avenue and passed a small car mechanic's garage that looked like it'd been a house at one time. The place was unique. I saw only Volkswagens there so I told Bernie about it. He said we'd give it a try for our VW's tune-up.

When our appointment time came, I asked Bernie not to call our Beetle his "Nazi Footlocker," as he liked to do for a laugh.

"These guys might not like your sense of humor," I said.

The mechanics who worked there belied the casual look of the place. They were all experts, the kind of men Bernie liked and respected.

After we'd been in Saint James for three years, I was reading through a stack of *New Yorker* magazines I'd picked up at a garage sale, delving into the cartoons first. It was then I saw it—a hilarious cartoon of our sleepy Lake Avenue car repair garage, depicted by a terrific cartoonist named George Booth. Unbelievable!

In Booth's hands the place morphed back into a lazy-daisy operation, complete with scruffy cats hanging around. I laughed out loud. From then on, I fell in love with the place, Booth's cartoons, and the *New Yorker*.

Bernie and I on vacation.

The house we rented on the edge of the Hartman Potato Farm had once been the home of the farmer's son. Azaleas lined the driveway. Five-foot hydrangea bushes hugged the windows. Our backyard tableau consisted of a climbing tree massive enough to hold our kids and their cousins, a sandbox made of an old tractor tire, and a background of potato fields, all looking sewn together like a methodically planned quilt. The scene belonged in a Norman Rockwell painting on the cover of *Look* magazine, and it was ours!

Bernie moved out of his apartment on Long Beach and into our new place. He loved wearing his white Pan Am flight engineer hat and was overjoyed with the job and his easy commute to JFK.

Two years later, when Oma and Opa offered to watch the kids in Chicago for a week so we could take our first Pan Am trip, I couldn't wait. It was January 1969, and we were finally traveling together to Europe. We'd spend a few days in London and then meet Jim and Sandi in Rome.

I should have known my life would be full of adventure, no matter where I lived or where I went. And there it was—a remarkable surprise as we approached the plane. I hated saying a silent goodbye to London Town but figured I'd be back someday. As we boarded the 707 Pan Am Clipper at Heathrow Airport, the captain recognized Bernie and heartily shook his hand. After introductions, as we settled into our seats, he came back to invite us into the cockpit for the short flight to Rome. There would be no navigator on this flight so he said Bernie could sit in the navigator's seat—and I could have the jump seat.

Usually, the jump seat, the pull-down seat behind the captain, was offered to other pilots "deadheading," or flying as a passenger to pick up their next assignment in another city. Often it was where the Federal Aviation Administration (FAA) inspector sat when he surprised the crew, stepping aboard with his clipboard and checklists. But that day the jump seat was all mine. I was agog.

Bill, our captain, was a big bear of a guy with an oversized sense of humor. He pulled down the jump seat for me. I sat my trembling body down, took a deep breath, shut up, and listened.

Bernie sat at the navigator's table, next to the flight engineer's place. My eyes drifted to all the switches running along one wall, up over the ceiling, and down to the throttles and gadgets between the captain and first officer. I had seen these controls drawn on rolls of paper when Bernie was studying his engineering guides. Now they stood out in 3-D. I was impressed.

Bernie introduced me to the engineer and first officer, who were inches away. I saw how these men with different titles worked together like an orchestra with the captain as conductor. Watching this process was a once-in-a-lifetime opportunity. I willed myself to pay attention to every detail.

What a crowded, little, neat closet the cockpit seemed. Everything was in its place. I barely had enough room to cross my legs. *Pilots don't do that sort of thing*, I thought. Bernie the Engineer used to tell me how the stewardess would call him back to fix the coffeepot or tinker with the air-conditioning. Now I knew the real story.

The guys were busy with the checklist. I was busy noticing. Suddenly, I was perched atop a rocket. The power and acceleration on takeoff thrilled me. No more knocking knees.

"Put on your earphones," the captain signaled. *Aye aye, captain.* I loved hearing the copilot talking in code to the tower and the tower answering in faraway-sounding spurts. *Don't ever forget this, Sarajane. As Dorothy says, you're not in Kansas anymore.*

I topped over the Swiss Alps from the catbird seat as we maneuvered through the whipped cream clouds like a silver bullet. When we neared Rome, the captain told the tower in his phony Italian accent, "*Buona sera*, this is, eh, Clipper 21, app-roaching."

Big Bill morphed into Sid Caesar before my eyes. I asked myself, *Is he for real or is he kidding?* I turned to Bernie, who was shaking his head and smiling. I thought, *If the captain's just kidding, maybe these Italians on the other end will love this guy.*

The plane's engines ginned up with a whoosh of power, which took me aback. We descended to see the lights of Fiumicino Airport. Sudden, the air controller said insistently, "Clipper 21, go around. Go around." I sensed things weren't quite right.

With a nod to the copilot and engineer, Big Bill pulled a lever back, mumbled something to the crew, and pointed the plane skyward, straight to heaven. *Wow!* The crew came alive. As we circled in a wide arc to get into position for another landing attempt, the copilot shook his head as if to say, *Those Italians, no sense of humor.*

I remember Bernie telling me during his training how important these "go arounds" were: they upped the blood pressure and woke you up to the what-ifs of reality. If you were just about to land and the runway was blocked, you had to take it up in a hurry, circle around, and get in position to land all over again—a maneuver that took plenty of practice.

Bernie told me later that night that this go-around was a payback to the captain, who had dared mock the air controllers' language.

Never was I so happy than when my feet hit the ground and we said goodbye to Big Bill.

"You shouldn't have worried," Bernie said before dinner at the hotel bar. "Bill flew bombers over Berlin. He doesn't intimidate easily." I learned that was his last trip before he retired, and he was making the most of it.

Ever since, when I board a plane, I glance in the cockpit to see who might be sitting in the jump seat. If it's a woman, she's a pilot, not a pilot's wife. And if I pass by the captain when I disembark, I always comment on the landing.

"Any landing is a good one," Bernie used to say, "especially if you end up with the pointy end facing forward and can manage to walk away from it."

In those early days Bernie usually was the youngest pilot in the cockpit. Many of the captains were World War II veterans. On one transatlantic flight, the senior stewardess came to the cockpit to take meal orders. She took the captain's order, the first officer's, and the navigator's. In those days they had a choice on the menu and the steaks were broiled in the galley to pilots' specifications. She then turned to Bernie. As he was about to order, she put hand on hip and said with a grin, "Don't bother, honey. You're so young, I'm gonna *nurse* you."

That was one of Bernie's favorite stories. He had a bunch of them. As time went on, he found himself the oldest crew member in the cockpit and became nostalgic to think he was once that kid engineer who fixed the air-conditioning and made sure the galley coffeepots were purring. He especially liked telling the young new hires about the memorable stewardess who had a good time at his expense.

I wonder if the young guys ever believed him, or if they thought he was just one of those old characters showing off, another Captain Bill.

Chapter 13

FURLOUGHED

Furlough was the airlines' word for layoff. I'd never heard of an airline laying off pilots, but they did, even the prestigious ones. When hired, each pilot received a seniority number, considered as relevant as his Social Security number. In a way, it *was* his social security: He would be able to return to his airline when they recalled, if he kept his number. In the meantime, another airline wouldn't consider him if he still held his Pan Am number.

Bernie found out about the pending furlough in June 1970 as he waited in line at the Pan Am Credit Union. He was getting ready to withdraw money so we could put a down payment on a house. After renting on the Hartman farm for two years, we were excited at the prospect of owning our own place. Bernie told the flight engineer in line behind him about our house plans.

"Haven't you heard?" he said. "We're about to be furloughed. I heard we'll be getting our letters tomorrow."

"Tomorrow!" Bernie must have felt the blow as he stood there, trying to remain calm.

When he arrived home, I heard no happy, "Hi, hon, what's up?" Only silence, which wasn't like him. When he said he was being furloughed, I did my best to absorb the news. Bernie stirred martinis. We adjourned to the backyard.

We loved cocktail time out there, watching the international flights high overhead as they headed to JFK. That night we talked about our future and how relieved we were that Bernie found out when he did. We didn't need a new house, anyway. What had we been thinking? Farm life was good enough.

Bernie knew a pilot's wife who worked as a high school secretary. Occasionally, she called him to teach as a substitute, but it didn't pay much and would never lead anywhere. After a while he said it wasn't worth the paltry pay. He also said some of the girls came to school in one outfit and then changed into skimpy garments stowed in their lockers.

He told about a few "forward" girls who'd sit in the front row of his history class and hike up their skirts to embarrass him. I couldn't quite picture him reacting to that, but it must have been with humor. When *Raiders of the Lost Ark* debuted years later, we enjoyed watching Indiana Jones squirm when he faced a similar predicament. Only in his case, the girl wrote "love you" on her eyelids. Bernie's naughty students weren't nearly that clever.

Bernie was at sea without a full-time position. One furloughed pilot tried to talk him into selling insurance, but he said that wasn't a good fit. After a few months crept by, my impatience at his reluctance to find a permanent job surprised and alarmed me. Plus, I didn't know how to help him. I thought of going back to work and even inquired at the phone company for a service representative position. They weren't hiring.

My pilot was relieved to discover Air Dominicana was hiring Pan Am furloughed pilots and engineers. Their base of operations was the island of Hispaniola in the Greater Antilles in the Caribbean Sea. I knew Haiti made up one side of the island but not much about the Dominican Republic on the other side. Off Bernie went to be a flight engineer on the 707s along with a few other Pan Am crew members. They lived in an apartment that came with a cook and housekeeper. I was eager to take the kids there when they finished the school year, but it was not to be. A few months later the airline folded because of the unstable Dominican government. More disappointed than ever, Bernie came home.

One night a few months later, we were having cocktails with my sister Germaine and her husband, Tom. One martini led to two. I felt light-headed. Their house was part of a new development on what used to be farmland. We saw the kids playing on the farm road that ran along the other side of their backyard fence, and we began to discuss the furlough.

Our hosts tried to be encouraging, with sentences like, "They might recall any day now" and "Pan Am's reputation is at stake." Finally, Germaine said, "Why don't I ask my neighbor Dick if he would hire you? He heads a big construction crew."

"No, don't ask him," Bernie said.

I felt so discouraged, helpless. *If only he would communicate with me!* We needed a survival plan. I left the table and walked down the hall to the bathroom so I could cry, undetected. My big sister found me—a heaving wreckage, full of too many martinis— and we talked it out.

"I can't stand this any longer," I told her. "If he doesn't get a job I don't know what we'll do." This was so unlike him. *Where did this inertia come from?* I wanted to brush it away, like lint on a sweater, but I couldn't. Now, in retrospect, I see that a man's job defines him, and without it, his dignity may be lost, too.

Germaine walked over to the phone and called Dick. Yes, he was willing to meet Bernie.

"Send him over," Dick said.

After she hung up and told me what he'd offered, I looked at her with astonishment. She answered simply with her arms out, palms up, as if she were just as surprised with her new, take-charge role. I freshened my face. We walked back to the patio, arm in arm, to announce the good news.

Bernie was reluctant, as he'd been with everything else I'd suggested. But now even Tom insisted that he do something.

"Go on over. It can't hurt," Tom said. He grabbed a bottle of Scotch from his larder. "Take this, Bernie. Dick will appreciate it, I guarantee."

An hour later Bernie walked into my sister's house, smiling, and told us about his new job. He'd be digging trenches and laying pipe for the completion of the Long Island Expressway in Riverhead—an easy commute. He seemed energized, even elated. We were, too.

Our hosts accepted our thanks with hugs and kisses, and we gathered up Lisa and Paul for our short drive home. The cozy red house on the Hartman Farm never looked so inviting.

Bernie had a union job. He belonged to the Laborers' International Union of North America. It pulled us out of the fog of instability and gave my pilot his dignity back.

We lived on the farm for four years. Our landlord, Mr. Hartman, was kind. He plowed a vegetable garden for us, gave us tips on what to plant, took the kids on pony rides, and let Paul climb all over the old, unused tractors outside the barn. Bernie kept the old ranch house in tip-top shape, painting the interior and making the basement into a playroom.

After a year of digging ditches, Bernie seemed a new man. Each day he wore his old boots and air force fatigues, stripped of rank.

"You were in the air force for five years and had no stripes?" one of his fellow workers asked him. "You must have been a real screwup!"

Bernie loved to tell that story. I'd never seen him so fit. His biceps bulged. His sun-bleached hair grew long. Four-year-old Paul noticed a change, too. Instead of a white Pan Am hat, his dad was wearing a hard hat, one that Paul could try on without worrying about getting it dirty.

When a work crew parked outside our house to pave the road, Bernie took Paul out to talk to the man working the front-end loader. They chatted and the man let Paul sit in the driver's seat.

After they said goodbye, Paul turned to his father.

"I knew you'd be one of those guys someday, Dad," he said.

Lisa entered kindergarten at Mills Pond School, down the street. I liked the quaint neighborhood school. So did she. Paul attended nursery school at our church, and I spent time there, helping out when I wasn't taking classes at the State University at Stony Brook, a few miles across the potato fields. I had completed two years at Coe College before we were married and wanted to gather more credits toward an eventual BA degree.

Sitting with Lisa, Paul, Rudy and Gretel at our house in the Hamptons.

I looked forward to Rudy and Gretel's visits, which were usually in the spring or summer. Gretel taught me how to can tomatoes and peaches—something I never thought I would or could do. The kids played outside while we took over the kitchen on those canning days. This gave my mother-in-law a chance to share stories about her childhood in the old country.

133

Gretel told me how she loved growing up in southern Germany in Lobenstein, a small town near the Thüringian Forest. She was the baby of the family, the youngest of three girls, and her talents for homemaking skills were well known.

"Every week," she said, "my mother sent me to a special lady in town who was known for her fine needlework skills—crocheting, knitting, embroidery, and needlepoint. I learned everything I could."

That morning we'd brought back three baskets of peaches we'd picked from a local orchard. I watched as Gretel scalded them in piping hot water. Then we slid off their skins and sliced them into the Ball canning jars. This would be the first time I'd have a store of home-canned tomatoes and peaches in the basement. It all looked so easy.

As Gretel sterilized the canning jar lids in boiling water, the steam loosened tendrils of her silky, strawberry blonde hair. She wore nylon stockings and a girdle under her housedress "to strengthen my lower back muscles", she said. (She'd had a back operation in her thirties and it still plagued her.) Beyond that stocky, hausfrau image and the wear of sixty years, there stood the true Gretel in her comfy, bedroom slippers. She was a woman in her element—a kitchen, one that just happened to be her daughter-in-law's kitchen. She was absorbing my gratitude as she taught me how to become like her and passed down techniques I needed to please my family. Gretel had already taught me how to knit, and now I was canning fruit!

As I saw her at work, I pictured a young German girl as she appeared in the Giere scrapbooks—a standout beauty compared to her sisters, a girl who liked to pose for the camera and clown around with her gang of friends. I couldn't imagine my father-in-law acting like that. He was from Bremen in northern Germany, the more sophisticated area of the country, according to Gretel.

Bernie's parents met in Chicago at St. Paul's Evangelical and

Reformed Church. Rudy was a chauffeur for a wealthy widow. Gretel was a nanny for an Irish family.

"Tell me again how you met Rudy," I asked her. By this time, the peach jars were boiling on the stove and I was writing down the recipe so I wouldn't forget. Gretel wiped her hands on her apron and laughed.

"He saw me acting in a church play and asked to meet me," she said. "When I said, yes, I would go out with him, he asked if I would mind waiting another week! Do you believe that? He had a bridge tournament to attend to first, but I said I'd wait, and I did."

We looked forward to our meals when Rudy and Gretel were with us in Saint James.

Mid-air refueling over Nam.

One late afternoon, Bernie came home from his union job with good news. He had just learned from a friend that the air national guard in Brooklyn flew tankers and they were looking for pilots. That serendipitous conversation led to Bernie joining the 106th Refueling Wing at Floyd Bennett Field in Brooklyn while he worked on the expressway.

Guardsmen flew one weekend a month, sometimes more. This flying job sounded great—the perfect complement to Pan Am—because if and when he was recalled, he could keep his part-time guard position.

The KC-97 Aerial Refueling Tanker was a plane the air force pilots appreciated, Bernie told me.

"Nobody kicks ass without tanker gas," he said.

In March 1972, when an opportunity came to move up in the guard ranks, Bernie grabbed it, becoming the full-time flying training supervisor of the 106th Refueling Wing. I wasn't surprised about the promotion. My pilot's talents and abilities were easily discernible.

"As a GS 13, I'll be making $18,737 a year—big bucks compared to highway labor and not bad for a lowly government job," he said.

We were thrilled. He hung up his hard hat and put on his flight suit.

For the next two years I accumulated four course credits at the State University at Stony Brook and began assisting in Paul's nursery school. I hoped to finish college someday, so I'd have the credentials to land a good-paying job if our circumstances called for it. I never took our life plans for granted anymore. So I wasn't surprised when Bernie walked in the door one spring day and announced we were moving again. He took off his boots in the utility room and didn't greet me, as usual, as he entered the kitchen

"Well, honey," I said, "what is it?"

"Sarajane, I have good news and bad news. Which do you want to hear first?"

"Good news, of course," I said, thinking it must be a Pan Am recall.

"I'm going for F-102 training in Houston with Pete. Our tanker unit is being transitioned into a fighter-interceptor squadron. I'll be on active training status for six months with the 147th Fighter Interceptor Group of the Texas Air National Guard at Ellington Air Force Base."

"Great," I said. I'd heard of these fighter jets that flew in Vietnam and I saw Bernie was holding his enthusiasm in check for my sake. "Tell me more. What's the bad news?"

"I'll have to move to Houston for six months. You all can join me for the last three months, after the kids finish up the school year," he said. "And you'll have to arrange the move by yourself."

"I can do that," I said.

Bernie explained he would rent a two-bedroom duplex for us near the base. In October, when his training was up, we'd all move back to

Bernie in the cockpit of the F-102.

Long Island but to the East End. The air guard was leaving Brooklyn and moving to the former air base at Westhampton Beach.

"We should move out there, too. It's the Hamptons, you know," he said. "It's beautiful. You'll love it. Lots of landscapes for you to paint. New house, new school, new job."

How could I refuse? It had been two years since Bernie's furlough in 1970. This would be the sixth aircraft Bernie would master—a single-seat supersonic interceptor, the F-102 Delta Dagger. The plane was built as the backbone of the United States Air Force air defenses in the late 1950s. Its main purpose was to intercept invading Soviet strategic bomber fleets during the Cold War.

We learned something important while we lived in Saint James: the path to the plum position of Pan Am captain would be a slippery one; but if, along the way, your survival plan included a permanent flying job with the air national guard, you didn't have to worry about what came next.

Chapter 14

HOUSTON TO THE HAMPTONS

Lisa, Paul, and I marshaled our luggage and shuffled out of the air-conditioned Houston airport terminal to wait for Bernie. We plopped on a bench.

"Phew. The heat comes at you," six-year-old Paul remarked. "Wham. Right in the face."

"You got that right," I said. "Welcome to Texas."

My toes prickled. I looked down to check my sandal and found a huge, black bug exploring my foot.

"Yikes!" I shot up, stamped my foot, and shook him off while Lisa and Paul stood, gaping. The critter kept going, but I was too upset to smash him. I composed myself.

"Everything's bigger in Texas, kids," I said, "even the roaches."

Bernie arrived. We took turns kissing and hugging. Paul described the gigantic roach as we piled in the car. *A former West Texan like me should be able meet foot-crawling roaches and not complain.* I sank into the copilot's seat and turned up the air-conditioning, relieved and happy to have my captain take the controls. The four of us were together again. It felt wonderful. Nine years earlier Bernie and I had left Big Spring. There we were, back in the Lone Star State.

Our pilot regaled us with all the amenities awaiting us in Clear Lake City, a community he discovered that was a short drive from Ellington Air Force Base. NASA was nearby, and the town contained all we needed—shops, schools, libraries, a sports center, entertainment, and a recreational area with tennis courts and swimming pools. Bernie had rented a two-bedroom duplex that would suit the four of us. Sparse as it was, our furniture had arrived the day before. This all sounded promising.

"The astronauts send their kids to the same school Lisa and Paul will be going to, so it must be pretty good," Bernie said, as we drove into our new neighborhood. Our handsome salesman continued. "You kids can ride your bikes to school. It's hot, I know, but there are compensations—three swimming pools within a few blocks of us, and you can walk to the Dairy Queen, too."

Our street, Silver Pines Avenue, hummed with life. Across the street, construction workers drilled, hammered, and nailed up frames for more homes. The man next door revved up his motorcycle each morning for his commute to the space center. Our new city, a modern planned community, was worlds away from Saint James.

We liked the liveliness of the place. The walls were thin, but who cared? We'd be gone in four months. Our few pieces of furniture fit snugly in our spartan but modern duplex, which had two bedrooms, two bathrooms, and an open kitchen.

It didn't take long before our neighbor's teenage daughter, Nancy, introduced herself and her dog, a Great Dane named King.

"So that y'all can get acquainted," she said.

A perfect gentle giant, King examined the kitchen counter as if he were comparing it to his own. When his tail wagged, it whipped a thump, thump against whatever was nearby. Lisa and Paul couldn't get over how Nancy kept saying "yes, ma'am" or "no, ma'am" when I asked her a question. I saw that Nancy and King would be a unique babysitting team—two for the price of one.

School started on August 15th, which drew sour faces from Lisa and Paul. But when the time came, they adapted to it. Bernie fit in his new squadron like he'd always been there. I could tell he loved it by the stories he told about the friends he'd made. Flying the supersonic F-102 must have felt like being in the F-4 Phantom again.

My first proof that our place was bug infested was when a palmetto bug, also known as a flying cockroach, swooped out of our kitchen cabinet right over my head. I ducked, yelped, and ran back to bed.

The next time an airborne creature startled me during the night, I chased the little bugger until I squished him with Bernie's boot. Then I left him and the boot there all night, as proof the next morning that I wasn't exaggerating. The spiders were big babies, too, but the natives never complained. They were on a first-name basis with their exterminators. When we left in October, I knew the guy, too.

On weekends we four covered Houston and Galveston as tourists, watching the fishing boats come in, touring NASA, fishing in the bayous, visiting the outdoor theaters, and cooling off in the Galleria—the huge, enclosed shopping center that boasted the largest ice rink in Texas.

My sister Germaine called to suggest I contact her friend Bunny who owned a summer house not far from the old Westhampton Beach air base where Bernie would work when we returned.

"Bunny lives in Manhattan," my sister said. "She says she'll rent you her summer house for the winter." I called Bunny and was overjoyed at her proposal. The rental price and location seemed perfect.

"Of course! I'll rent you my place," she said. "The house will be rather chilly in the winter, but it's a beautiful location. You'll love it. Moriches Bay is at the end of the street and it can be windy. You'll have to vacate by Memorial Day, the start of our summer season."

"It sounds wonderful, Bunny, and your price is right. It'll be nice to know there will be a place waiting for us in October. What a lifesaver you are!"

After Bernie completed his training in October 1972, we drove up to Long Island, making a quick stop in New Orleans. I was so happy to see my sister and brother-in-law in Stony Brook. Germaine and I talked nonstop into the night. Her three kids and our two were delighted to be together again; they formed a little squadron of their own and entertained us grown-ups and each other.

After we left Germaine's we drove straight to Bunny's. The drive was a palette of colors—trees burnished with gold and scarlet, sign-cluttered roadside farm stands, and pumpkins nestled in their green farm beds.

Bernie reported to the 106th Fighter-Interceptor Wing at Westhampton Beach while we settled into our new place, which was a short drive from the base and ocean beaches. The small elementary school was right down the road.

The quaint clapboard house waiting for us on Shore Road lacked insulation, but it had a fireplace, well-stocked bookshelves, and a bar in the dining room. The plush sofas were stuffed with feathers, which, along with the dust-blowing heating system, would prove to be the bane of Paul's allergy episodes.

My neighbors told me Alfred Hitchcock once lived in this quaint little hamlet. So did P.G. Wodehouse, who collaborated on the musical hit, *Anything Goes*, with his neighbor, Guy Bolton. These greats were gone as well as most people, it seemed, as I stood in the middle of Shore Road one fall afternoon and peered down to Moriches Bay. *Where is everybody?* There was not even any mail delivery, only post office boxes. Now and again I'd see someone walking or riding a bike to pick up mail. The exclusive enclave seemed asleep. I supposed that's why the celebrities liked it.

On February 12, 1973, three months after we arrived, an afternoon TV report jolted me back to our Vietnam days: the first POWs were returning home. The first sixty men from the large group of 591 prisoners disembarked at Travis Air Force Base in California.

I cheered for the wives and children who embraced their men after they stepped off the plane and saluted the commander in charge. Bernie could have been one of them. I was thrilled to recognize our friend from pilot training, Bert Campbell, walking proudly from the plane. He looked the same, only thinner. Bert earned two silver stars as a F-105 pilot. He ejected over North Vietnam only two months before Bernie was shot down. He was captured and imprisoned for seven years. After his release we lost touch with him. Later we learned he led a distinguished career in the air force until his death in 2003.

How lucky we were to have Bernie back. His return was the gift of a lifetime. If those men could endure such captivity and walk off that plane, Bernie and I had nothing to complain about. Our problems were insignificant in comparison.

I unearthed a letter Bernie wrote me while he was at Coe College and I was in Saint Louis living with my parents, working at the telephone company and saving my $62.50 weekly paychecks so we could afford to marry. In his letter Bernie comments about a movie he and his fraternity brothers had seen: "It was on prisoners of war, and the thing to do is to keep one's mouth shut. I surely hope I never have to fly in a war because it will be hell."

Five years later Bernie crouched in the field of elephant grass in North Vietnam, watching the Jolly Green Giant hoist Jimmy into its belly. As he waited for it to circle around and rescue him, he must have pictured himself a likely prisoner of the Viet Cong. He joked about it many times in the years to come. Fighter pilots are like that. His squadron mates kidded him about how loudly he squawked on his radio, "Hey guys, come back, come back. There's another one down here!" No matter how he framed it, the rescue proved a defining moment in his life. Every setback he experienced from then on must have seemed less daunting.

I read everything I could about these released POWs. Their resilience astonished me. My cousin John G. Hubbell wrote *POW: A Definitive History of the American Prisoner-Of-War Experience in Vietnam, 1964-1973.* To historians who want to know anything about those captive men's' stories, John's book is known as "The Hubbell."

The POW return made all the news stations. There were pretty stewardesses on the giant C-141 that brought the men back.

"We have stocked the plane for you," one gal told a returnee. "You can have anything you want. What would you like?"

"I'd like a Coke with crushed ice, and chewing gum," the fellow said.

Later we learned that one former POW said he'd always wanted a nose job to correct his hooked nose. He got it.

Another soldier remarked he saw a miniskirt for the first time among the families waiting on the tarmac.

The next few years would be quite an adjustment for these men. When I look back at those riotous years in the '60s and '70s, I see the breathtaking size and scope of the Vietnam experience and how it changed all of us who lived through it. Bernie and I had served our country through our different roles. He tested himself in the field of combat and survived, feeling stronger for it. My theater of operations was at MacDill Air Force Base as I grew confident assuming the role of an air force wife and single mother to Lisa and Paul.

I prayed more during those times than all my previous years combined. I felt God was there for me when I needed Him the most in 1965 and 1966. I realized how vulnerable and impatient I was and that I needed to be more forgiving of myself and others.

The many months my pilot and I spent apart also showed us the strength of our marriage and our love for each other. From then on, especially during Bernie's furloughs, we knew any trials to come would pale in comparison to what we'd endured in wartime.

While I walked past the lovely Remsenburg homes, *en route* to pick up Lisa and Paul at school, Bernie was launching his second career in the air national guard. I thought of myself as a seasoned veteran, more mature than contemporaries I knew who hadn't been close to the war. *Do the people who live in these houses behind the hedges know someone who served in the military or even in Vietnam? What they think of Vietnam shouldn't be my concern,* I told myself. I was just glad Bernie was back in uniform, and I hoped the anti-war protesters wouldn't mar the image of our military or affect the pilots stationed with the 106th in Westhampton Beach.

We didn't realize it then, but Bernie and I were shifting from one reality to another. My pilot had been through an incredibly difficult experience, but for some of our old friends, life was the same as it'd always been. "There is so much they don't know," Bernie told me, "and so much they don't care to know."

The first two women I met at the kids' school had daughters in Lisa's class. When they asked me to lunch the following week, I was surprised.

"We're your informal welcoming committee," they said.

I was flattered. Later I wondered if I should have been. After a few rounds of conversation, I realized they were sizing me up for entrance into their world—a world that wasn't mine. By admitting I was from Saint Louis, I felt I was automatically tossed into yahoo land. No New England pedigree there. And yes, my husband was, of all things, military.

The prospect of starting over in a new place always gave me a lift. I thought of those welcoming committee gals as I continued to the school, mulling what my place in this new universe would be. I knew it wasn't with them.

My walk down Shore Road took me past the Bouvier compound, owned by one of Jackie Kennedy's distant relatives, Kathleen Bouvier. I peeked through the hedges to the peeling columns at the front entrance. Though surprisingly shabby, it was a pillared entrance all the same. I assumed that counted for something in the Hamptons.

There were one hundred fifty kids in the K-6 school—less than half the size of the Houston one the kids had attended. I walked into the lobby. The principal stood near the main office and watched the kids line up. He wore a tweed sport coat, a button-down shirt, and penny loafers like the ones Bernie preferred. His expression was that of a doting father.

"Hello, Mrs. Giere," he said. "We're so happy to have Lisa and Paul with us. Have you settled in yet?"

I knew then that this must be the right place for the kids, especially when Lisa told me about the punishments doled out in her Clear Lake City fourth-grade classroom.

"If a student misbehaves," she said, "the teacher pins a tail on him and says, 'You go stand in the corner!'"

As I unpacked books for our winter rental, I flipped through my *Air Force Wife* manual, only to find that the very sayings I'd made fun of a few years earlier seemed genuine now. The first chapter was entitled *"Esprit De Corps,"* which means "the spirit of the body or group." Author Nancy Shea wrote that the keys to the United States Air Force were its range and change, which in technical terms meant mobility and adaptability. That didn't sound like military dogma anymore. That was us!

While I scouted out permanent housing, Bernie continued as flying training supervisor with the F-102 squadron. The 106th was a rowdy bunch of pilots from all over the East Coast who'd moved to Westhampton to join the unit. It seemed like pilot training all over again. The dinners and parties gave us all a chance to get acquainted, though, and most of the restaurants appreciated the business, especially in the middle of winter. There was one exception, the Continental Bamboo, which banned us from returning.

The restaurant, accustomed to quieter clientele during the winters, hadn't seen the pilots' "Dead Bug" drinking game before. It was rough on chairs. Someone yells, "Dead Bug!" and then falls backwards over his chair to the floor. The rest of the guys do the same. Kaboom! The guy who goes down last has to buy drinks all around. On the night I remember, the last man didn't go down. He stood, looking down at the others on the floor.

"This is a new leather jacket," he said. "I don't want to ruin it."

Pilots are an odd bunch sometimes.

Meanwhile, I wasn't having much luck finding the right house. As the weeks ticked by, I got nervous. Then one night at a PTA square dance, we met Ray, a contractor who told us about a "spec" house he'd just begun to build one block from the school.

"Can we see it?" Bernie asked.

"Sure," Ray said. "It's a two-level house on a quarter acre that I'm selling with the downstairs interior unfinished. It's the right price for a quick sale."

The lot was in a wooded area of modest cottages and quiet streets. Perfect. The little community by the Speonk River had served as a welcome retreat for city folks in the '30s and '40s. Many of the original homeowners were still there.

Ray's scrub oak wooded lot sat on a corner where two streets met at a dead end. As Ray gave us his pitch, we walked over the foundation slab and tried to imagine the layout. The property was atop a small hill, which gave a promontory-like view of the surroundings. Bernie liked the idea of finishing the downstairs himself. Knowing how meticulous he was, the kids and I teased him: "There's the standard way of building and then there's the Giere Way."

The property overlooked the river, which wasn't more than a big stream. Ray told us Speonk was an Indian word for "high place." That's where our future house would sit, offering a view of the woods across the street and, behind, the little river that led to Moriches Bay and the Atlantic Ocean beyond.

Speonk River

In back of the property lay an abandoned duck farm. The tops of the long, narrow barns peeped through the trees. Bernie turned to Ray.

"I don't know about living next to a duck farm," he said.

"Sarajane can paint it," Ray replied.

He was right. Eventually, I did, immortalizing those weather-beaten barns—and even selling the paintings—until a hurricane took them all down a few years later.

Ray said the house would be finished by the end of May. We bought it for thirty-five thousand dollars, a bargain for the area, and moved in the week before Memorial Day. From then on, we considered the Hamptons our home.

From our treehouse perspective we saw the river and its surrounding wetlands, echoing a brilliant sunrise painting by Monet.

Herons, kingfishers, and graceful snowy egrets lived there. The swans, our permanent residents, took us by surprise if we sat outside. Their explosive liftoff lasted a few seconds and then they soared above us, their whooshing wings pumping in unison. They gave me goose bumps. Bernie liked to explain the aerodynamics of the takeoff: gravity pushed their wings higher the faster they flew. We learned not to get too close after their goslings were born. Those awkward siblings were prey to the snapping turtle who hid in the tidal shores of the wetlands.

We heard the old turtle was an expert at stealing swan eggs. Six-year-old Paul and his friend Ronnie must have overheard us talking about it, for off they went, unnoticed, through the woods and down to the river's edge. Bernie and I sat on our patio with Ronnie's parents, Ginny and Ron, telling them about our lovely new neighborhood, which I called "Nature's Window."

The boys came trudging from the woods holding the creepy snapper. Yikes! Its head reminded me of a miniature Godzilla. That monstrous face with its gaping mouth could take off a tender boy's hand in an instant. Didn't they realize?

"Hey, look what we found," the kids said, as if it were a prize they'd just won.

The men told them to put it on the ground and got an empty paint bucket. They had the boys push the turtle in. Bernie put a hot dog on the end of a stick and ran it under the creature's nose. Snap! There went the hot dog and most of the stick.

While their fathers lectured, the boys nodded in agreement, promising to stay away from the river, but I knew it was the hot dog demonstration that convinced them. Back went the turtle as we continued our barbecue.

Bernie and I grew to love our new Remsenburg home. We realized that even the most modest of dwellings in the Hamptons could command a spectacular view. Ours delighted us.

Few pilots I knew at the air national guard base were inclined to do construction work during their time off, but to Bernie finishing our newly built house would merely be play. A few months after we moved in, our neighbors noticed Bernie setting up his sawhorses in the driveway to begin work on the downstairs family room. The first to stop by was Richard Vitzius, an elderly man in threadbare tweeds wearing a tartan cap and a belt made of rope. I saw him riding his bike toward our yard and went out to meet him. As he approached, he smiled, donned his cap, and said, *"Wie gehts?"*

Bernie grabbed the old man's hand.

"It goes well with us, *Guten Tag,"* he replied. The old man smiled. Here was Richard Vitzius, known to his friends as "The Professor," a German-American we came to know and respect. Bernie said Richard reminded him of John Piltz, his godfather, who would have been Richard's age by then. When Bernie was growing up, his parents' German friends called him Bernard, and he spoke German fluently until he entered kindergarten in 1944. He remembered his mother pulling him off a bus before they came to their stop and saying, "Never speak German on the bus again. People don't like it."

Richard became an American citizen in the 1920s, built a fulfilling life for himself, and then retired in a cottage he and a friend constructed from the ground up in 1946. He was in his late seventies when we met him and rode his bike to the post office every afternoon. We eventually discovered he'd authored four books. My favorite was *How to Make Your Fondest Dream a Pleasant Reality*.

He taught us about the area and why the duck farms were disappearing.

"The Long Island Duckling has seen its heyday," he said. "With these new environmental regulations, it's hard for farmers to survive."

"I've been sketching those dilapidated barns," I said. The professor smiled.

"Good. Better get them before they disappear. That property is worth millions when the farmer decides to sell." Bernie's gaze met mine. He smiled.

"I always said this neighborhood had potential, honey." I knew he must have been thinking of me and my painting plans as well as the increase in property values for our little house. A million dollars? Next door? Wow! I hoped the property wouldn't be divided into lots while we lived there.

That first year while the kids were in school, I explored the duck farm property. I was delighted by how the late afternoon sun changed its shadowy designs on the barns, day after day. I loved the geometric structures of those long, narrow barns and their rooftop cupolas. The vines that snaked through and around the broken windows looked as if they'd been purposely placed to enthrall an artist's eye.

The sight of Bernie in our driveway drew other company to-ward him, including Jimmy Suka, who lived nearby. Jimmy and Richard Vitzius were buddies. Once they brought over some bourbon. The three fellows had their afternoon cocktail sitting atop the railroad ties Bernie had fashioned. They held up the flower bed that rose from the driveway up to the front door.

Jimmy told Bernie he suffered from "shell shock" after Korea and had spent time at the Long Island VA hospital. We were sympathetic. Jimmy and Bernie talked about the Korean War, Vietnam, and the new air guard mission with the interceptor jet fighters, the F-102s.

Jimmy's mother was a Swedish immigrant who tended three pet geese in her backyard. She liked to invite Lisa and Paul into her kitchen and give them goose eggs and handfuls of crumbling cookies wrapped in newspaper. Years later Lisa told me she saw ants crawling in the Sukas' refrigerator so she never ate the cookies.

I knew the poor old woman was on a journey to senility the day I saw her walk across her lawn to the street and then sit primly on her suitcase with her purse in her lap. We never figured out what Mrs. Suka was waiting for. After a while she usually gave up and went back inside.

"My mom thinks she's going back to the Old Country," Jimmy said, as if this made perfect sense. Perhaps to Jimmy, it did.

Another original, Pete the Greek, a dapper, flirty old fellow, lived down the block in a cottage distinguished by a homemade grape arbor in his backyard. It was full of special Greek grapes, he said. I never saw Pete without a carnation in his lapel or a stash of Jolly Ranchers in his pocket. He walked to the post office to check his mailbox and lingered in the lobby until he met someone he recognized who might give him a lift home. Since I drove there often, I had a substantial collection of Jolly Ranchers, jokes, and gossip to digest. Friendly Pete was quite a character. O. Henry would have put him down on paper, word for word.

Five years later, Mr. Vitzius became so weak, it worried me. I began taking dinner to him. Sometimes he met me at the door. Other times I let myself in and found him in his favorite over-stuffed chair. One night I was horrified to see him sitting in the chair, soaked in urine. He apparently couldn't get up to go to the bathroom, and that's when I asked myself, *What would Bernie do?* He always seemed to be on a trip when I needed him most.

I called my doctor, who examined Mr. Vitzius and pronounced a stroke. I called my pastor. He came, too. The doctor called the police, who sent a patrolman. I was surrounded. The policeman said I would be responsible for Richard; someone had to sign. I saw no other option.

Eventually the ambulance arrived. The attendants put Richard on a stretcher and carried him out the front door. The Professor's jumbled words of protest made no sense. He pulled his wool cap down over his face and defiantly crossed his arms over his chest, as if to say, *I dare you.* The poor soul probably knew he'd never return.

He spent three months in the hospital. I visited him there many times and, at the nurse's request, brought a suitcase packed with his clothes. When Richard was transferred to a nearby nursing home following his hospital stay, his suitcase didn't travel with him.

"It's disappeared," the nurse said.

A few months later, Mr. Vitzius died. Richard had outlived most of his friends. The local chapter of the Odd Fellows took care of the Masonic service and burial. I was surprised and impressed by this kind gesture.

Around that time Mrs. Suka also died, and Jimmy was admitted to the VA hospital. After we moved to East Quogue seven years later, I occasionally saw Pete the Greek on Mill Road where he liked to hang out near Westhampton Beach Cleaners to greet the customers.

PART 4

"Barn's burnt down — now I can see the moon."

— Mizuta Masahide
17th century Japanese poet.

Chapter 15

AIRLINE SIDELINE

When Pan Am recalled Bernie in November 1973—after a three-year hiatus—we were ecstatic. We were settling into our new Remsenburg house, the kids were in their new school, and Bernie was flying international runs on the Boeing 707 as well as with the New York Air National Guard.

A mere two months later, at the end of December, we received a Christmas present from Pan Am—Bernie's second furlough notice. Why? The gas crisis, according to the airline. Pilots thought it was just bad management.

We were aware of the gas shortage that began in October 1973 when members of the Organization of the Petroleum Exporting Countries (OPEC) proclaimed an embargo targeted at nations perceived as supporting Israel during the nineteen-day Yom Kippur War. Of course, we waited in the long lines at gas stations, too, but we never expected the crisis to affect the airlines. Those behemoths of transportation seemed invincible.

Bernie showed more resiliency with this layoff. He was a F-102 Delta Dagger pilot and proud member of the oldest flying unit in the air national guard, organized in 1921. He readily accepted a full-time job as air technician and worked with highly trained and motivated people. The guard was the best place to burnish my pilot's talents and reward him for his contributions.

Often Bernie sat at his desk, scribbling in a spiral notebook as he recorded dates and other statistics he thought significant. He was a detail man, like his dad. In Chicago Rudy sat at his "secretary," an antique upright desk with shelves above for books, cubbies for incidentals, and a pull-down desktop for letter writing. Rudy, the writer of the family, also was a keen draftsman who, as a twenty-seven-year-old immigrant, worked his way up from chauffeur and welder to engineer—without credentials. He designed and created meticulous cardboard prototypes for new tools and machines at a large manufacturing company.

Rudy had hoped to return to pharmacy, his profession in Germany. Sadly, as a young immigrant in the late 1920s, he had no money to pay for either night school classes or the required pharmacy license. Rudy didn't let that setback define him, though. I saw the same resiliency in his son.

My pilot was proud of the drafting skills he'd learned in high school. Before we married, he drew on graph paper a complete layout of the apartment he had rented for us "for only $100.00 a month." I still have it and wonder if any high schooler today could match it.

Bernie made lists of our trips together; our former addresses, ten in all; and every family member's Social Security number. It seemed to me that by recording significant events, my pilot was paving his way forward in life, summing up his progress as he went along.

My pilot, who recorded every flight he ever took on eleven types of aircraft, kept many logs of his flying hours. Each was a dog-eared, pocket-sized notebook that had seen plenty of wear. His Vietnam missions numbered 214. His flight hours added up to hundreds more. His resume kept growing.

Even when Bernie was challenged with the first stages of ALS, and his hands gradually lost their coordination, he sat at his desk and, in his vertical handwriting, filled in his medical note-book. As I discovered later, he made many lists of things I needed to know once he was gone. I didn't realize until after he died that he had recorded years of doctor visits for what he thought was a herniated disk problem in his lower back.

We lived in the house that Ray built for five years. Bernie's folks visited often. They flew from Chicago, bringing a frozen marzipan cake from the Swedish bakery on Clark Street and a loaf of Lithuanian Rye Bread. We thawed out the cake to celebrate an upcoming birthday or anniversary. In the years since, I've never found a cake that matched it, which makes it No. 1 on my German Foodie Dessert List.

When our neighbors moved to Ireland and sold us their thir-teen-foot sailboat, Bernie brushed up his sailing skills so he could take his dad out on Moriches Bay. I had no talent in this arena but was mighty glad I married a con-fident swimmer who could ma-nipulate a boat. When Bernie was twelve, he and his dad made a two-man kayak from a kit. They hefted it down to Diversey Har-bor in Bernie's wagon and had some fun. Watching them hoist the sail at the boat slip in Rem-senburg charmed me. They were father and son, at it again, on the water.

Bernie sailing with his father, Rudy in Remsenburg slip.

In August 1974 Pan Am is-sued a recall notice. We hadn't expected that. The furlough had lasted eight months. We were on the seesaw again, but this time we were on top.

Once again Bernie transitioned back to a part-time national guard position and flew the F-102 when he wasn't flying for Pan Am. Three months later the airline promoted him to check engineer. No surprise to me. He commuted daily to JFK to check out engineers in the simulator and in flight. He was even on the seniority list to make first officer, which means copilot.

Shortly thereafter, the 106th transitioned from F-102 fighter jets to Aerospace Rescue and Recovery. Bernie learned to fly the C-130 Hercules, a four-engine turboprop military transport aircraft designed in 1954 to transport troops and cargo. At the time it was said to be the most important aircraft in aviation history.

We heard a C-130's four engines lumbering overhead before it came into sight, and I liked that. Some local residents loudly complained about the C-130 Hercules to Air Commander Giere. They said their wine glasses danced around their barroom shelves and crashed to the floor.

"It's unfortunate they bought a house near the end of the runway," Bernie said to me. "What a great clever realtor they must have had."

In its role with the 106th, the Hercules C-130 performed aerial refueling during search and rescue missions. It also had spotters aboard to look for shipwreck survivors in the ocean. Once they were noticed, pararescue jumpers, or PJs as they were known, jumped or parachuted from the plane. They could also jump from the HH-3E helicopter, the Jolly Green Giant, an integral part of many rescue missions.

Bernie liked and respected the PJs, who were lively, competitive men. The minimum requirements for the job were to run one-and-a-half miles in eleven minutes, swim sixteen hundred yards in under an hour, and swim twenty-five yards underwater.

There were only two rescue units in the air national guard—the 106th in Westhampton and its sister unit in California. After the midair explosion of the Space Shuttle Challenger in 1986, the 106th Rescue Wing was chosen to provide support for every shuttle launch thereafter. One C-130 and two helicopters, along with the rescue team, would be at Cape Canaveral and in the air during each liftoff.

More commonly, rescues were at sea. The first occurred in 1976. By 1986, the rescue and recovery crews had made two hundred "saves," mostly rescuing the crews of floundering fishing ships or sailors aboard smaller vessels.

Bernie flew the Boeing 707 until the third and last furlough arrived in 1976. This layoff would last ten years, but we didn't know that then. Bernie thought his chances of being recalled again were slim but, just in case, he kept his Pan Am number. He never attempted to quit and work for another commercial airline. From then on, he devoted himself to the air national guard.

Because of his managerial, problem-solving, and piloting skills, Bernie eventually moved up to a full-time lieutenant colonel position as air commander in December 1977. Eight years later, as group commander, he oversaw the entire operation, supervising a workforce of eight hundred guard members.

Remsenburg's old houses intrigued Bernie. After completing the downstairs of our home, he wanted to find a fixer-upper we could live in—a place with a history, one he could restore to its old glory.

He was itching to get hold of some two-by-fours. I had discovered just how much he loved building things during the first year of our marriage, when we saw a pine, drop-leaf, end-table in a furniture store and thought it would go well in our living-room. I wanted to buy it, but Bernie deferred.

"Let's wait until tomorrow," he said. He never made a quick decision. The next day we returned so Bernie could take notes and measure the piece.

"Keep the salesman distracted," he said, pulling a small notebook and pencil from his pants pocket. I couldn't believe he had the nerve, but he seemed to know exactly what he was doing. The next day, my happy husband turned the dusty, cramped space under the eaves of our attic apartment into a workshop where he built a perfect replica of the little table.

"How ingenious," I said as I placed a lamp on the glowing, finished product. The table, having survived five moves, proved its usefulness over the length of our marriage.

Bernie in the cockpit of the C-130.

Eventually, after four years, we found an old place on Remsenburg's Main Street, a short walk from our neighborhood. The one hundred-year-old summerhouse had a wraparound porch and a barn out back but little insulation. Its radiators hissed and pinged. The cellar had a dirt floor and its *Little House on the Prairie* stove begged for renovation. We bought it and rented our ranch by the river to a family from the guard.

The kids wanted a dog, but Paul's allergies to pet hair limited our choices. Our spacious backyard led to the woods. The kids and I felt it would suit a dog just fine. Bernie felt differently. Nevertheless, Lisa and I found a year-old Cockapoo named Baby at the Westhampton dog adoption center and brought her home. We told Dad that Paul would be allergy free around a half poodle, half cocker spaniel mix. We knew he'd grow to accept her and he did, especially when we discovered she'd already been trained to sit, heel, and chase a ball. Baby was with us for fifteen years.

The biggest snowstorm in decades came along in February 1978. Snow fell at four inches per hour. Winds gusted to 60–80 mph. Digging a path from our kitchen door to the car had to wait while Bernie stayed at the base and sent rescue trucks to travelers stranded on Route 27. Then he oversaw the safety of the base equipment and tended to the needs of the guardsmen camped out there.

Finally, he came home, driving the airport's snowplow and telling tales of eight-foot snowdrifts. Bernie seemed to know instinctively how to handle this maelstrom, making me and the air national guard personnel feel safe.

C-130 Hercules in action.

Hurricanes also kept Bernie busy: The pilots took the helicopters and planes to other bases for safety. Meanwhile, Bernie and his staff implemented emergency plans that impacted the community. Once a fire in Westhampton threatened the base. Bernie also settled union disputes, hosted dignitaries, made speeches, and prepared for Operational Readiness Inspections (ORIs). My pilot spent most of his time "flying a desk" when he wasn't flying the C-130.

One fine day in June 1978 the sun filtered into my tiny art room. I rearranged my easel and opened the windows. The kids were with friends. It was Wednesday, my day for painting. The kitchen screen door clapped shut. Then I felt Bernie's hands on my shoulders. I felt a chill. He wasn't due home until five o'clock.

"What's wrong?" I asked, turning around.

"We lost a helicopter."

"What?" *This can't be true. They're all seasoned pilots.*

"Went into a mountain. They were on their way home from a training mission in the Adirondacks."

Bernie sighed. I put my arms around him and laid my head on his chest. He felt solid, unshakable, but I could tell by his heartbeat that the stress was building. He patted my back and kissed me. Then he pulled away and turned toward the stairs. I followed.

"Were there any survivors?"

"No."

He named the dead—two pilots, both Vietnam veterans; a flight mechanic; a crew chief; one PJ; and two staff sergeants in their early twenties. I fought back tears. *These are our friends who are supposed to save lives, not lose their own.*

"I'm going with Nick to let the wives know," Bernie said. Nick was the pilots' squadron commander.

"Do you have to?"

"No, but I want to."

"I want to be with you," I said. He seemed surprised.

"All right. You can come. That would be good."

We climbed the stairs to the bedroom in silence. Bernie eased himself down on the edge of the bed, exhausted.

"Please bring me a clean shirt," he said.

I reached in the closet and grabbed a fresh uniform shirt and laid it out carefully on the bed while I dressed in a hurry.

"We're ready," Bernie said, facing me. He kissed my cheek. "Thanks for coming with me."

There it was: whatever happened, we were stronger by two.

Bernie, Nick, and I drove to the homes of the two pilots to tell their wives. There was no script for the scenes that lay before us. I trusted the good Lord to prompt me. Bernie was silent, introspective. The men talked in low tones.

Jacquie Sfeir came first. I liked her because her ways were kind and gentle. Her four-year-old twins tagged along behind her as she answered the door. Jacquie's older son was at a school for children with special needs. I was glad he wasn't there. She took one look at us and knew bad news was coming. I stayed back as Bernie and Nick approached her.

I told the kids to play in the family room while we talked. I ushered them in, then turned back to Jacquie. She was running her hands through her hair. She looked startled. At first she smiled. Then she looked at Bernie and Nick suspiciously.

"What's going on?" she whispered, backing against the wall.

"It's John," Nick said. She cupped her hands over her face. Nick went to her.

"Oh, no," she said, "this can't be."

Bernie said there'd been a crash and how sorry he was. He held out his hands and drew her up so she faced him. She held his hands for a moment. The tears came. She turned to Nick to reassure her, as if there'd been a mistake.

"I'm so sorry, Jacquie," Nick said. "We don't know the exact circumstances yet, but we do know there were no survivors." She was wide-eyed with horror, as if the accident was unfolding in front of her.

"Who was the other pilot?" she asked. Bernie told her. She breathed deeply, then asked about the rest of the crew. One by one, after each name, she let out a mournful sigh.

When Bernie finished, Jacquie said, "Oh, dear God."

"We'll all be here to help you through this, Jacquie," Bernie said. When I hugged her I felt the tension in her body.

"I'll take the twins outside," I said, turning toward the playroom. "Hey, kids, your mom is talking to some friends from the base right now. She asked me to take you outside so you can show me your swing set."

I put the kids on the swings and entertained them with stories I pulled out of my childhood. Their backyard gradually slanted downwards to a pond, where two swans preened. *What a wonderful place this is. How happy John and Jacquie must have been when they first saw it.* I glanced through the family room windows and saw Bernie put his arm around Jacquie as she held her head in her hands. Nick walked over and gave her a glass of water. He was talking to her.

"Your mom has to meet with the men for a little while longer," I told the kids. "She'll be out soon."

The scene at the swing set seemed to go on and on. My chatter flowed out automatically, but underneath it all, I felt one with Jacquie, a lovely, gentle woman who didn't deserve this. I wondered how I'd react if it were Bernie instead.

Finally, we were called into the house, which grounded me into the reality of the situation: *You're here in East Moriches at Jacquie and John's house, and you have a job to do.* Jacquie made some phone calls and then sat at the dining room table with the men. I took the kids into the kitchen and asked them to help me make sandwiches, but it was no use. They sensed something important was happening in the other room.

After a few friends came, we left. Bernie said Jacquie wanted to know who was flying the helicopter—in other words, who was at the controls.

"It couldn't have been my husband," she said. "John was a such a careful pilot."

"We don't know anything now, Jacquie," Bernie said. "It's still early."

Our next visit was to the wife of the other pilot, John Kleven. Bernie and Nick wanted to tell Kvet about John before the accident appeared on local newscasts. As we drove, Bernie told me that three years earlier, John's dad, an airline captain, had died in a crash at JFK. I took deep breaths. This visit was getting harder and harder to envision.

Kvet was shocked to see the two uniformed pilots, both friends and colleagues of her husband, at her front door. I stood behind.

"Don't tell me he's dead!"

"I'm sorry, Kvet. John didn't make it," Bernie said. I saw the disbelief in her eyes and heard it in her denials. Overcome, she turned away.

Bernie and Nick told her as much as they knew about the accident. She, too, asked who was flying the aircraft.

"It hasn't been determined," Bernie said.

"It wasn't my John's fault," she said.

I've often wondered if Bernie knew which pilot was flying at the moment of the crash. If he did, he never acknowledged it to me.

While Kvet paced the living room, I thought, *Oh, my God! The agony of grief.* I wanted to hug her to show I cared, but I didn't think she'd accept the gesture. Not then. I told her how sorry I was and tried to comfort her. I made tea. She called her sister.

As Nick and Kvet talked, Bernie and I sat on the sofa. I was glad John's two-year-old son was napping upstairs. His bright crayon drawings were displayed throughout the room. They reminded me of the ones our son, Paul, drew at that age. I wanted to cry. My pilot sensed how uncomfortable I was. He laid his hand on top of mine and gave it a squeeze. The warmth of his touch shot through me.

167

When Kvet's sister arrived, we once again expressed our condolences. Bernie and Nick assured her the air national guard members would be there to support her in the days ahead for as long as she needed them. I trailed the men to the car, thinking what a life-changing event had just taken place in a matter of minutes.

The next five days passed quickly as the staff at the headquarters of the 106th readied for the arrival of the caskets. On June 16, 1978, a humid, hot day, fellow airmen, other armed service groups, relatives, and friends stood quietly as the C-130 lumbered up to Base Operations. Bernie was inside, meeting with family members who'd been sequestered with him and other base officials and dignitaries. Local media waited for them to make an appearance.

As the group walked resignedly from headquarters to the tarmac, Bernie had the air of one long accustomed to such duties, a built-in strength for these occasions. I was proud of him.

An air national guard band played "Nearer My God to Thee" as two groups of pallbearers carried each coffin from the plane to a row of dollies in front of the reviewing stand. The seven were presented with full military honors by base personnel of the 102nd and 106th units. During the service a rainbow appeared over the runway—a symbol of warmth and reflection for many of the friends and families since then, according to Chief Master Sergeant Tim Malloy (Retired).

Speeches were made. The governor bestowed the state's Conspicuous Service Medal awards posthumously. Relatives and friends wept and comforted one another. One guardsman fainted from the heat, or emotional strain, and was carried from the tarmac.

Afterwards, during one of the four burials at Calverton National Cemetery, I wondered how many other military interments I'd witness in my lifetime. The relatives clung to each other as they watched the guardsmen stand at attention. I looked beyond them to a sea of tombstones, unrolled toward the horizon—all those white markers, standing in perfect formation, just like soldiers.

I thought of the many young men who gave their lives for their country like the twenty-two-year old staff sergeant we honored at that moment. They were, all of them, buried along with their hopes and dreams. I wondered if I'd die leaving any hopes for my life unfulfilled. Life was short and unpredictable. I was thirty-eight and had always wanted to finish my degree. *I'll do it—and soon*, I promised myself.

Two guardsmen removed the American flag from the coffins, folded each ceremoniously, and presented it to the family. The sound of "Taps"—the familiar, plaintive farewell that always brought tears to my eyes—filled the air. I grabbed Bernie's hand as we walked away. I knew this burial was more significant than the others and that my life, from then on, would take a different turn.

After that day, I often thought of my gravesite promise and its outcome, especially when I saw the simple granite monument displaying the list of the fallen crew members from the helicopter crash. It was dedicated the year after the incident and still stands today. When I passed it on the way to Bernie's office, I paused to read the names. It always humbled me to think my twenty-three-year teaching career came as a result of such tragedy. Yet, I told myself, my promise probably wasn't the first one made at a graveside.

As hectic as the next three years were for us, with Bernie working full time at the guard and Paul and Lisa wending their way through junior and senior high school, I returned to my studies at the University at Stony Brook. I earned a bachelor's degree in Fine Arts and went on to earn a master's degree in Education at Southampton College. With certifications in four subjects, I readily found a job teaching reading and art in nearby Riverhead.

Chapter 16

TRAGEDIES AND TRIUMPHS

My architect, absorbed with his flying and supervisory duties, began to rue the day he thought he'd have time to update the old house we bought. My biweekly laundromat visits were getting tiresome, especially in wintertime. And we all knew our place on Main Street was uncomfortably cold and ill-equipped for the long run.

We decided to move into the twentieth century. Luckily, in 1980, we found a home in East Quogue, a village in the kids' Westhampton School district that was closer to the base. A local builder bought our Remsenburg farmhouse and immediately dug a proper basement and remodeled the barn.

When Bernie was recalled to Pan Am in 1986, we had a difficult time processing the change. We were certainly grateful and happy but also wondered how long the job would last. That year would be a pivotal one.

My friend Betsy came to live with us for a year until she could get her life together and find a job and place of her own. I hosted many out-of-town guests when our daughter, Lisa, married Tom, a wonderful Long Island lad. Paul attended Coe College in Cedar Rapids, leaving Bernie, me, and Betsy at home. With Betsy willing to mind the house and the dog, Bernie and I were freer to travel than ever before.

After Bernie became copilot on the Atlantic routes of the A-310, we took several trips to Europe with Jim and Sandi. Those were travel-packed years, each adventure offering stories to record and remember.

We four visited Mexico, Hawaii, France, Italy, England, and Africa. When we were in Mexico City, we took time to drive to Taxco, a small city known for its silver mines and jewelry shops. Sandi and I held hands and closed our eyes as our old, cramped rental car motored upward on mountainous roads without guard-rails. As we approached Taxco, several tour guides stood by the side of the road and shouted for us to stop. We did. Bernie and Jim got out to talk to them. Soon one of the men folded himself into the driver's seat. Bernie sat next to him while Jim made a place for himself between us gals. Oomph!

"Hang on," Jim said. "this guy's taking us to the best silver shops."

As we sped up the steepest road I'd ever seen, I thought of all the roller coasters I'd avoided my whole life. My heart thumped. I didn't throw up. We survived. Bernie paid the audacious driver and we ended the day with a few silver jewelry pieces that didn't seem worth the torturous overture.

Whatever predicaments we got ourselves into, Sandi and I trusted our pilots to get us back on track. If they survived Vietnam, they could get us through any crisis. Usually, we even ended up laughing.

And then, on December 5, 1991, Pan Am World Airways ceased operations after sixty-four years because they couldn't raise enough cash to keep flying. The airline was losing an estimated three million dollars a day, according to industry sources. I was crestfallen when I heard the news. I recalled the early days of Bernie's Pan Am career when he came home from one of his first trips in 1967. He told me about a distinguished passenger he'd met—Charles Lindbergh, who then sat on the airline's board. Bernie was impressed. So was I. If Lindbergh believed in Pan Am, it would last forever. Or so we thought.

Jim, Sandi, Bernie and I in Paris, 1990.

The Pan Am collapse had a surprising outcome. Delta Airlines—a Southern airline that Bernie used to call Mother Ferguson's Storm Door and Airline Company—bought Pan Am's Atlantic routes along with its A-300 series airplanes and their pilots. Since Bernie was a first officer—copilot—on the A-310, he was one of the lucky ones. He flew for Delta for the next ten years.

Bernie's job as air commander at Westhampton left him time to fly for the airline, but his full-time position of group commander did not. This problem was solved when he was bumped up to full colonel and became deputy head of operations for New York. The post came complete with an office upstate where he reported at least a few weekends each month.

The change allowed my pilot to balance his two jobs. Even after he turned sixty in 1999, and by law could no longer sit in the pilot's seat, he went back to being a flight engineer with Delta. That way he accumulated enough years for a pension he never fully received from Pan Am. The transition to Delta seemed effortless.

"I just took off my white hat and put on the black one," Bernie said.

That same year, 1991, tragedy struck the 106th again when it unsuccessfully attempted to rescue the Andrea Gail, a commercial fishing vessel ultimately lost in the Atlantic Ocean with all hands. Author Sebastian Junger wrote about the incident in *The Perfect Storm*, released in 1997. A movie of the same name followed in 2000.

The storm began as a tropical low—the merging of hurricane remnants from the tropics and a strong system over the Canadian Maritimes. It was listed in histor-ical records as an "unnamed hur-ricane" and in later years was lik-ened to Superstorm Sandy, which raked the East Coast in 2012.

Colonel Giere

The 106th got a disaster call and dispatched a rescue team. In such a storm, though, the C-130 Hercules could not perform the midair refueling. The helicopter crew could not refuel from the C-130 because of turbulence, so it had to ditch in the ocean. All but a PJ aboard survived: the rest were picked up by a coast guard vessel.

I was glad Bernie wasn't part of this fateful attempt. Losing another helicopter pilot was a blow to the guard. Because of the popularity of the book and film, the unit gained notoriety for the mission and the heroism of its rescuers.

Most missions of the 106th were successful. Bernie was at the controls of the C-130 during a notable rescue in December 1979. The unit saved nine lives aboard the John F. Leavitt, a 97-foot, wooden-hulled schooner on its maiden voyage from Quincy, Massachu-setts to Haiti. The vessel ran into trouble 268 miles southeast of Montauk Point in a storm that brought heavy winds and enormous seas. By the time the helicopter and the C-130 reached the vessel, the Leavitt was very low in the water and listing to portside. The ship's 100-foot masts precluded an on-deck landing. Instead three PJs jumped from the helicopter into the water. The crewmen were already standing in waist-high water, but all were rescued.

The survivors expressed their gratitude to the air national guard: "From our position on the rolling deck, we were impressed by the obvious organization and training of the paramedics and the aircraft crews. It takes a special type of person to extend them-selves to voluntarily take part in an operation that puts their lives in jeopardy."

Layover in Nice with Bernie and the cockpit crew.

Another well-documented rescue occurred in December 1994 when two helicopters from the 106th rescued a Ukrainian sailor from the Salvador Allende 750 miles off the coast of Nova Scotia. After the C-130 flight engineer spotted a waving figure, the helicopter banked sharply and hovered ten feet above water. Two PJs jumped from the helicopter into waters where sharks had been spotted only one hundred feet away. One PJ swam to the Ukrainian sailor and hoisted him up into the helicopter.

During the grueling fifteen-hour mission, each of the two helicopters required ten air refuelings from a C-130 in 60 mph winds and driving snow; two were performed after dark using night vision equipment.

Many awards were given for this feat, among them the American Helicopter Society's Kossler Award. It recognizes the greatest achievements in practical application or operation of a rotary wing aircraft.

Although not unheard of, it's rare that a rescuee becomes a rescuer. In a few words, that's the irony of Bernie's twenty-four-year career with the 106th. He was furloughed from Pan Am for a total of fifteen years, but the air national guard rescued him. It gave him another chance to fly and return the lifesaving favor for people in distress on land and sea.

In a 1981 newspaper interview, Bernie said, "It's just a thrill for me to be in Rescue, the perfect mission for the air national guard. I always get a lot of satisfaction when I see a helicopter return from a mission."

Bernie harked back to his own rescue in 1966, when a rescue team lifted him into the bowels of the Jolly Green Giant helicopter in Vietnam.

"I figured it was now or never," Bernie said. "The bad guys knew where I was because of my chute, so I popped smoke and directed the crew to me. Everything went perfectly. It was a picture-book rescue. We were shot down, on the ground, and picked up all within an hour."

When interviewed at age forty-six, upon assuming the title of air commander, Bernie said, "I still get excited about this rescue mission, as do all of our people. It is a real mission, and far from routine. The call can come at any time. We are given an opportunity to serve and practice what our shoulder patch says, 'These Things We Do That Others May Live."

Bernie always felt flying for a major airline would be his most satisfying career. Yet it was with the air national guard that he experienced the most fulfillment and became an inspiration for others.

Chapter 17

RUDY COMES ABOARD

Bernie and his father, Rudy.

A horrendous fall and two-week hospital stay in 1999 finally convinced Rudy, at age ninety-three, to leave his independent lifestyle in Chicago and move in with us.

Five years after Gretel died of a stroke in 1982, he'd moved into Leisure Village, a high-rise apartment community for seniors. He loved it for many reasons: He was near his old neighborhood and his church. He enjoyed a view of Lake Michigan from his apartment window, and he could play bridge every day. We visited often and thought it was the perfect place for him.

Our daughter Lisa, her husband, Tom and their two daughters, lived in the Chicago suburb of Wheaton. Opa Rudy loved to visit them by train. Lisa and the girls would meet him at the Wheaton train station once a week. This routine visit soon became the highlight of Rudy's week, and a special day for Lisa and her girls. Eight years later, after Lisa, Tom, and the girls moved to New Jersey, and with Paul and his family living near us on Long Island, we hoped Rudy would move east, too. He refused.

The fact that Rudy lived alone at age 94 and took public transportation to Wheaton each week worried Bernie and me. A few years earlier he'd fallen in his apartment and banged on the floor to alert the tenant below. He'd been lucky to survive that mishap with no major injuries.

When Carol, the administrator of Rudy's place, called Bernie in August of 1999, to say Rudy had fallen a second time, we knew something had to be done.

"I'm sorry to tell you, Mr. Giere, that we've lost our electrical power here at Leisure Village because of the unprecedented heat wave," she said. Your father fell and fractured his elbow and has broken some ribs," she said. "It could be worse than that, I'm afraid. He's in the hospital now."

Bernie put the phone on speaker mode for me.

"What exactly happened there?" he asked.

Carol explained how Rudy had tumbled down a flight of stairs, trying to get his newspaper from the lobby.

"We had warned our residents to stay put because of the power outage," she said. "We planned to escort them down to the lobby to be bused to the nearby Hilton Hotel, which had power. It seemed Rudy had decided not to wait for his escort. He tried going down the stairs himself."

"We'll be there as soon as we can catch a flight out," Bernie said.

"I'm so sorry this happened, Mr. Giere."

"I am, too." Bernie hung up, turned to me, and heaved a sigh like a father would after hearing bad news about his wayward, teenage son. "I can picture him, can't you?"

I nodded as I sat down to listen while Bernie meandered through Rudy's frontal lobe, where logical thinking is supposed to take place.

"Dad was probably missing his *Tribune* and that big Sunday crossword puzzle," Bernie said. "He didn't want to wait, so he thought he'd walk down thirteen flights of stairs to get it from the lobby."

"Thank the Lord he only toppled his way down to the next landing," I said. "We can be grateful for that."

Bernie cracked a smile and glanced down at his overburdened calendar.

"How's about a high-octane trip to Chicago?"

I was on my summer break from teaching, but Bernie had only a few days before leaving for training on the Airbus A-310, another large passenger plane he'd be flying for Delta.

We packed, made a few calls, and caught the next Delta flight to Chicago. After Bernie and I settled into our seats, we massaged the jackpot question as we nursed our drinks: what are we going to do about Rudy?

As we discussed options, it became evident that Bernie was now the parent. Rudy was the child. We had work ahead of us.

By the time we arrived at Leisure Village, electrical power throughout the city had been restored. We checked in with Carol, who led us to a guest apartment that was ours for the duration—a pleasant surprise. Doors along Rudy's hallway sported pretty wreaths, name plaques, or welcome signs. Rudy's door was different. Nailed in the center was the Rube Goldberg cardboard contraption that held his newspaper.

Rudy was well acquainted with cardboard after all those years designing mock-ups for machine tool designs. After he retired, he created household cardboard problem-solvers for a grateful Gretel.

Saint Joseph's Hospital was three blocks from Leisure Village. Both fronted Lake Michigan. This was the Near North Side of the Windy City, Rudy's territory for more than seventy years. Convenient to Chicago's transportation center, Saint Paul's Church, and the lake, it was no longer a German immigrant neighborhood of row houses but a prosperous mix of apartments, individual homes, stores, and parks.

Rudy told us he liked to walk to Saint Paul's.

"What about in winter?" I had asked him.

"If it gets too windy," he replied, "I just put a paper bag over my head and cut holes for my eyes!"

We were glad to hear Rudy's injuries weren't life threatening. The CT scan showed no brain damage. He was glad to see us, and we were happy to see him smiling through all the medical paraphernalia encompassing him. The doctor was attuned to our situation and heartened by Rudy's positive attitude.

Back at Rudy's, we dug through his private life, reluctantly at first. Bernie opened Rudy's checkbook for the first time and discovered his father liked to sign up for advertising offers—hundreds of dollars' worth. We found drawers of half-full jars of supplements and vitamins and stacks of *Reader's Digest* tapes and gift books piled high along the baseboards.

"He shouldn't be living like this," Bernie said, shaking his head. "Dad can't live alone anymore."

I agreed wholeheartedly, scanning the room for more surprises.

"The problem is, he doesn't want to move and lose his independence."

The day before Bernie left for Atlanta to begin his Delta training, he spoke to Rudy in his authoritative colonel's voice.

"Dad, when I get back here in two weeks, we're going to take you home to live with us," he said. "It's a done deal. You can't talk us out of it."

Rudy lay with his bandaged arm pulled up to a bar, his ribs wrapped in gauze, and one huge, purple bruise covering his forehead.

"Bernard," he said, "you know you can't replant an old tree."

"Yes, I've heard that before. We're planting you at our house. You'll have your own room. You'll love it. You'll see."

Rudy took a deep breath.

"Hmm. Okay. You go to training. Have a nice trip, Bernard. I'll be ready."

Bernie kissed him and left the room just as an officious nurse entered. Rudy tossed me a smile.

"This is Becky," he said. "She's a good girl, come to check up on me."

I thought to myself: *He'll get over this hurdle, just like he's conquered all the others in his life. Who knows? Maybe his last years will be his best.*

I soon began working through the apartment, making piles of clothes and everything else that was left of one man's life. Each day I opened Rudy's mailbox to find it chock-full of ads. When I saw the glossy come-on for Viagra, accompanied by a handwritten note to Mr. Giere, I wondered if he'd bought that, too.

Rudy's kitchen table sat next to picture windows that coaxed my eyes toward Lake Michigan. The white sails of the harbor boats glided purposefully, perhaps vying for first place in a sailing race. It seemed a perfect respite for a man who grew up along the Weser River in Bremen, Germany. I was gratified Rudy had enjoyed ten years with that view.

I moved boxes from Rudy's closet and set them on the table. There were a myriad of interesting items, including engineering and drafting tools, carefully asleep in their black velvet, elongated cases like strings of pearls in a jeweler's showcase. To Rudy, I supposed they were pearls. There were big fat keys and tiny, intricate keys tied together—keepers all, reminding me of ones I had known. There were also a few rocks worn smooth; a petite blue box of Shaeffer B-Fineline THIN pencil leads in tiny yellow metal boxes, costing twenty-five cents each; and erasers, four to a cylinder, that still worked after fifty years. Also keepers. The red, thumb-sized metal box containing five Schrader valve caps stumped me. I'd have to wait to ask Bernie about those.

I counted thirty packs of playing cards, stacked next to many German books, mostly written by philosophers such as Goethe and Schiller, as well as *Man in God's World*, a book in English by Helmut Thielicke. I'd keep them all.

I felt relaxed and respectful as I sorted the items into piles and wondered which remnants to leave behind. During those two weeks in Rudy's apartment, I thought of the week I moved my dad to a smaller apartment after my mom died. I'd learned by error how to make decisions—what to keep, what to discard. After my father died twelve years later, I tried to pack my sadness away with each box I filled. But it was no use. It took years to assuage the loss of my parents.

Now Rudy was my parent and I needed to concentrate on his welfare and happiness. He wouldn't see this beautiful view of Lake Michigan anymore, but, living with us, he would be near the Atlantic Ocean. He could hear its roar from our front porch.

When Bernie and I married, his folks gave us a recording of Anton Dvorak's masterpiece, *The New World Symphony*.

"You're entering a new world," Rudy and Gretel said.

I grew to love the music, as I did them. And just as Rudy came to America, he would soon be entering a new world again, both for him and our entire family. Life is nothing but new beginnings.

I walked to the hospital each day and stayed with Rudy for several hours, taking breaks in the beautiful lounge that overlooked the lake. There I read one book, *Red Heart* by James Alexander Thom, with a curious intensity, as if I were on vacation with nothing else to do. Based on a true story, the tale is about a little white girl captured by Indians and raised as one of them. When her relatives found her more than fifty years later, she preferred to live as she always had, with her people.

Bernie and I looking at an F-4.

I hoped Rudy would let go of his former life in Chicago, too, when he joined us. I wanted him to know there'd be joyful new milestones to supplement the old ones he left behind.

Bernie and I spoke every day about my progress. He told me to remind Rudy that he would be accompanying us to East Quogue when he was released. The Lord must have been watching over us because, earlier that summer, we had renovated our place, adding two bathrooms and bedrooms to accommodate visitors as well as our kids and grandkids. It all seemed providential.

"You'll have your own room and bath," I promised Rudy. "I'll even find you some bridge buddies."

"Okay, okay," he said. "Dat's good."

Two weeks later, when Bernie returned from training, we took his dad from the hospital onto a Delta flight at O'Hare that went straight through to JFK. This took gumption since Rudy was weak and could hardly stand alone, but we did it. As he'd done all his life in tight situations, Rudy didn't complain. His nature was recuperative, perhaps the result of his boyhood years. At age nine, he helped his mother and sisters survive in Bremen, Germany, while his father fought in World War I.

During the *Kohlrübenwinter,* or turnip winter, the Germans in Bremen had no potatoes to eat—only turnips. Although farm produce was being sent to the war front, some farmers' wives managed to hide bins of potatoes, *kartoffeln,* for their own use, and to trade for sweeteners like honey.

Rudy's mother sent him to the countryside by train to barter her honey for potatoes. His persistence paid off the day he hefted his booty onto a crowded train back to the city. He entered a car where all the passengers sat on benches facing the middle. Seeing one open seat at the far end, Rudy pulled his sack along the floor to claim it. He sat down, grasped the neck of the bag, and pushed it between his legs.

When the officious conductor entered and noticed Rudy's *kartoffeln*, he said, "*Aufstehen* (Stand up)."

Rudy knew he wanted the potatoes.

"*Nein,*" he replied. The conductor insisted. Rudy shook his head. "*Nein!*"

Remarkably, several men stood up and yelled back at the bully, "*Heir Raus* (Get out of here). This boy and his potatoes are staying just where they are."

Some of the others stood with them and shook their fists. Seeing he was outnumbered, the conductor relented and huffed off. There was a stir among the passengers. Many kind words were directed to the boy who wouldn't give in.

I remember the time in the '80s when Bernie was interrupted at our patio barbecue by a phone call from a doctor in a small Tennessee town. Rudy was in the hospital with a blood clot in his lung. He would be okay in a few days.

"I'll be flying out tomorrow," Bernie said. "I'll drive him back to Chicago."

His dad had been seeing friends in Florida and was on his way back when the pain hit. He didn't want Bernie to worry, but the doctor insisted that his son be notified.

On the ride back, Bernie gave Rudy advice about traveling alone long distances. He invited his dad to move to Long Island and live with us, as he'd done many times since Gretel died, but Rudy again politely refused. He was independent and he wanted to stay that way.

My first task after we settled Bernie's dad into his new room in East Quogue was finding a live-in caregiver. We didn't want Rudy to be alone in the house while we were gone. I needed to return to my teaching job in a week, and Bernie was flying different routes each month. A friend at school heard about a woman who might be looking for work. She'd been a theater manager in Warsaw, Poland. I arranged an interview for the next day. Kasia was a perky gal with shocking red hair in a neat pageboy.

"Sure, I can take care of an elderly man," she said.

She looked intelligent and willing, and there was no time to waste. It wasn't long before we saw Kasia wanted something else out of life—anything more stimulating. Her complaints about Opa gathered momentum each day. Once she even said Rudy groped her. Knowing what a gentleman my father-in-law was, I knew the claim was preposterous.

School opened and I was back at work, wondering what we should do about Kasia. Opa never complained. Once, after I'd returned from an evening meeting, she confronted me with more of Rudy's misdeeds. I realized I'd hired a diva, not a caregiver. After a few months, Opa mentioned that he was tired sitting in Kasia's car. I figured out that Kasia had been driving Rudy to Southampton and leaving him in the car while she cleaned someone's house. She probably earned more on a two-hour cleaning job than twenty-four hours as Opa's caregiver. I was outraged.

When Bernie came home and learned what Kasia had said and done, we stood together as one and told her, "You're fired. Get your stuff right now and leave!" She called her husband, who came in a flash. He pulled his car onto our lawn, popped open the door, grabbed Kasia and her suitcase, and fled.

Over the eight years Rudy lived with us, we had ten live-in caretakers after Kasia. The average stay was one year! Most were educated women from Eastern Europe whom we liked. Beruta from Lithuania had been a chef. She combed the neighborhood for mushrooms and created delicious sauces for us. Beruta's nephew lived nearby. After she left us, he sent us her sister, Emma.

After Emma left, there was a gal from Russia and one from Latvia—the only other woman we fired. While Bernie and I returned from Lisa's house in New Jersey, we found evidence that the Latvian and her husband had entertained friends while Rudy slept and even helped themselves to our liquor cabinet. She wouldn't leave her room. When we pointed out the blood on the bedroom rug and mattress and a hole in the wall, she said her husband had gotten into a fight with friends. We were shocked. This scared me. If we called the police, I worried about repercussions from what Bernie called "the Latvian Mafia." Bernie fired her and called her husband to come and get her.

Our last employee was a Lithuanian named Irena, who stayed for eighteen months and became part of the family. She played cards with Rudy each day. Rudy's favorite was Kings in the Corner, a game he could master and play with his great-grandchildren. The game bored Irena to tears but she soldiered on, knowing her time could be better spent cooking and cleaning. One day Rudy took Bernie aside.

"I have to play cards with her," he whispered, "to give her something to do."

We smiled at that. I loved Irena so much that I hated to see her return to Vilnius. Like Irena, many of our caregivers left to go back to family in Europe, or another job nearby. Our caregivers gave me an earful of what it was like growing up under hateful communist regimes. Witnesses are the best teachers.

A few years after Rudy came to us, Bernie retired from Delta. I was still teaching then, and Bernie did the grocery shopping and took his dad to the library and the ocean. Even with Bernie's availability, we always had a caregiver staying with us.

Over those years Rudy's nieces and nephews and their children visited from Bremen. We embraced one another, the younger members translating for us as we entertained our relatives. Friendships were forged so Giere family ties would continue through the next generation.

Our family loved being with Rudy, our patriarch. On his one-hundredth birthday, my sweet father-in-law looked down at his elaborate birthday cake and beamed. There were ten candles, each one representing ten years of his life. He shook his head.

"Yes, Dad," Bernie said, "it's true. You're one hundred years old today. You were born in 1905, and it's 2005 now."

Rudy savored the moment. "If you say so," he replied, "it must be true."

As we gathered around him, I thought of how he'd changed in the past seven years since we'd brought him from Chicago to live with us. He'd been ninety-three then, playing bridge at the library once a week, putting together intricate jigsaw puzzles, and mentally working out the square roots of numbers when he was bored. Now, at one hundred and in a wheelchair, he'd lost most of his hearing and had given up bridge for simpler card games.

After Rudy turned 101, he hallucinated. He became disturbed during the night and fell out of bed. One night he sat on the floor and played with the wires beneath his hospital bed. When we found an empty box of chocolates, we knew caffeine must have had a hand in the episode.

Other times Rudy fell onto the floor, and Bernie, Irena, and I struggled to get him back into bed. We realized he was too heavy for us. Bernie had a bad back then, which later became severe.

In the meantime, though, we had to do something about Rudy. Our doctor recommended a nursing home not far from us in Greenport. It overlooked the Long Island Sound. We reserved a room.

When we told Rudy he'd be moving to a nursing home, he replied, "Do you have a rope?"

Bernie looked puzzled. "Yes, Dad, but why do you ask?"

"Because I want to hang myself!"

The comment shook us. I felt like we'd betrayed him. Finally, after talking it over, Rudy acquiesced, knowing it was the best solution for all of us.

My father-in-law seemed to like Greenport, an old whaling town. The nursing home was decorated with a nautical theme, which pleased him. He spoke Russian phrases to his favorite nurse.

She giggled and declared, "Oh, Mr. Giere!"

I thought he'd probably picked up some phrases from the Russian POWs he'd guarded on a farm in northern Germany during the war when he was a boy—phrases he'd waited ninety-two years to repeat with such gusto.

190

Eight months later, just two months before he turned 102, Rudy died in his sleep. He had stopped eating the week before and said he was ready to go. Bernie and I visited him every day toward the end. We said goodbye, not knowing if he could hear us. The last night we visited him, I turned to exit the room, but Bernie didn't follow. I looked back to see him kneeling down at his father's bedside saying his last good-bye—a tender gesture that has stayed with me. I should have gone over and joined him. I always wished I'd had the courage.

We received a call early the next morning to say Rudy had died in the early morning hours. His presence with us had been a gift and a legacy of love, perseverance, and faith. How fortunate we were to have him with us.

Rudy with his bird, Roland.

Chapter 18

STOP THE CLOCK

Bernie standing next to the "Yellow Peril."

The billboard at Republic Airport caught my eye: "Biplane Rides." It featured the image of a daffodil-yellow, two-winged aircraft with a red-and-white-striped tail, vintage 1939. Bernie noticed, too. I knew he'd always wanted to fly one.

"Now's your chance, honey," I said. "There's your biplane."

I wasn't going to let him say no. He glanced my way and turned into the parking lot. We'd passed Republic, a small Long Island airport, many times *en route* home from our daughter's place in New Jersey. That day, it loomed large. An unexpected adventure was exactly what my pilot needed. He was in the early stages of ALS, a creeping, incurable disease, but we didn't know it at that time. All I knew was that he was changing right before my eyes and we'd have to find out why. Soon.

What greater tonic in the moment, though, than a ride in a vintage airplane. It would lift him up and away from his growing helplessness and let him take command in the air. *Hallelujah!* Before, when the opportunity to fly an iconic aircraft arose at an air show, Bernie said, "Nah, they want too much money." He'd mastered eleven airplanes in forty-six years but a biplane wasn't among them. This experience was a box he hadn't yet checked on his aviation bucket list.

For the past five years Bernie, my soul mate of fifty-two years, had visited all kinds of doctors to find relief for the debilitating spinal and back pain that had caused him to retire early from Delta. Most recently, he was seeing Dr. Dale J. Lange, neurologist-in-chief at the Hospital for Special Surgery in Manhattan. But Bernie was still in a holding pattern.

We'd thought about ALS. We knew it caused weakening of the muscles but we didn't know much beyond that. I'd soon come to learn it was a neurodegenerative disorder that caused loss of muscle fibers and motor function. Without muscle power, a person can't speak, breathe, or even swallow normally.

I couldn't even pronounce "amyotrophic lateral sclerosis" properly until I discovered the meaning of each word in Greek. Amyotrophic broke down into "a," meaning without; "myo," muscle; and "tropic," nourishment. Lateral referenced the sides of the spinal cord where the nerves that nourish muscles are located. Last, sclerosis signified the scarred and hardened tissue in the diseased part of the spinal cord where healthy nerves should be.

To his dismay, Bernie found that writing with a pen had become a chore and handling his fork and knife had become a science. Was it merely old age? He was only in his early seventies.

Rather than grouse about it, he muddled through. Occasionally he mentioned pain and stiffness in his lower back—a common ailment. His mother had suffered chronic back pain. I think he assumed it was a burden he'd inherited and had to live with.

A year earlier I'd noticed my pilot walked differently. He favored one side over the other but attributed that to his disk problem. When someone who hadn't seen him in a year remarked about his unusual gait, my worries escalated. Lisa, Paul, and I woke up to the fact he had more than a herniated disk. Our children insisted we find the right doctor—a specialist.

Bernie's best friend Jim, who flew with him in Vietnam, had been diagnosed with Parkinson's six years earlier. Congress and the VA had recognized the condition as a military-related disease.

While researching possible explanations, Bernie discovered that veterans are twice as likely to develop ALS than those who haven't served in the military, according to Wendy Henderson's "Military Veterans Twice as Likely to Develop ALS" (*ALS News Today*). As a rule, it takes a year to make a final diagnosis. There is no cure. The average survival time is three years; about 20 percent of people with ALS live five years. Five percent will live twenty years or longer. In later stages, patients lose all muscle functioning and need ventilator support to breathe.

Aside from those eye-popping facts, I stayed up late one night watching Gary Cooper portray Lou Gehrig in *Pride of the Yankees*. Then I ordered Eleanor Gehrig's book, *My Luke and I*, perhaps steeling myself for what might prove inevitable. Medicine had come a long way in recognizing and treating ALS since Gehrig's death seventy-eight years earlier, but no cure had been found. This fact haunted me. I wished I'd turned off the movie. My pilot, the lovely husband I wanted to keep for the rest of my life, was now the man in the spotlight.

When Bernie and I walked into Republic Airport to inquire

about the biplane ride in June 2011, we suspended our disheartening thoughts of the future. I knew his self-image had taken a blow. I wanted him to opt for this extravagant four hundred-dollar airborne excursion.

The moment we met Tiny, the handsome, lanky, six-foot former Vietnam fighter pilot, I knew it was a "go." Bernie signed on for the Stearman aircraft, known to its trainees as the "Yellow Peril." He fumbled out his credit card while I called our son in nearby Westhampton.

Bernie and I with the "Yellow Peril."

"Get a move on, Paul," I said. "Dad's going for a biplane ride. Bring Kim and the kids. You've got to see this!"

This outfit, the Warbirds, was run by a few employees—three pilots, the couple that ran the business, and the line boy who refueled and cleaned the aircraft and assisted the pilots. We waited an hour before takeoff, so we browsed around the parked airplanes outside the office. Bernie looked over the yellow Stearman he'd be flying, knocked on its propeller, and kicked the tires.

That sturdy old plane was doing its best to show off for us. It probably knew how Bernie and I combed through antique stores and junk shops, looking for the best of the old. Through the years furniture with resumes had filled our houses before we graduated to non-useful items, such as an old, wooden propeller Bernie bought in California and had shipped home in a ski box. He loved its craftsmanship—the thin metal strips folded along the blade's edges, punched in place with bullet-like grommets. His father would have appreciated such a work of art.

"It's going over the mantel, Sarajane," Bernie said. "It's not the Rembrandt you wanted, but the next best thing."

An hour later Bernie was outfitted and ready to go. He was my Errol Flynn, the dashing, aviator hero of *Dawn Patrol*. Paul, Kim, and our three grandchildren stood with me as Grandpa strode out of the office. The chin straps of his leather aviator helmet hung loose while he toted a bulky vintage headset in his hand.

"Have fun!" we shouted, as Tiny and Bernie walked toward the plane. The line boy hoofed it alongside, carrying the copilot's seat pack parachute.

When we met at Coe College, Bernie walked me to class. Whenever we parted, I watched him continue across campus to Old Main. I loved that thin, muscular frame and his confident stride. He had a way of walking on the balls of his feet as if he were moving to some happy, internal tune. As I watched him near the plane, I thought I saw rhythm in his step again. *Am I seeing things? Has the old Bernie bounce really come back?* I hoped so, if only for a minute. His walk spoke volumes.

In order to contort himself into the front cockpit, Bernie needed help from Tiny and the line boy because he had scant muscle power. This insertion into the cockpit seat took patience, a quality Bernie had in spades. It pained me to watch him, though. As we waited for takeoff, my eight-year-old grandson Matt told me about the Stearman caps for sale in the Warbirds' office.

"We can buy Grandpa a Father's Day gift there," I said, giving him the thumbs up.

We all stood on the hot, windy tarmac, our grins wide and our iPhones poised for pictures. We saw Bernie in the front seat and Tiny behind him. The kids knew Grandpa was slowing down. But the malady didn't have a name yet, other than "back trouble." I, however, had been in a state of unspoken mourning for the last few years, watching the man I love gradually lose his muscle power.

That day the kids watched their grandpa struggle—poignant evidence he'd never return to the way he was when they were growing up. *If this is Bernie's last flight,* I thought, *I hope it's a doozy.*

Tiny glided the plane down the airstrip at 75 mph. Compared to Bernie's takeoff in an F-4 at 180 mph, this was child's play. I saw it was Bernie's moment to savor, though, as the yellow bird became a little toy.

The biplane glided to the end of the runway. I thought of the young pilots who'd flown the Stearman in an earlier era—Bernie's predecessors in the Triple Nickel Fighter Squadron. He was about to share that experience, which made the flight even more significant. When the plane finally went airborne, a sense of delight came over me—a tingling feeling of joy that oozed down to my toes. I wanted to stop the clock.

As he sat aloft in the front cockpit, behind the hum and thrum of the propeller, Bernie was where he wanted to be—flying again, in another world, three thousand feet above us. The plane flew out of sight. I was sorry not to see the rolls and lazy loops they executed, but we witnessed several touch-and-goes, a maneuver that involves landing on a runway and taking off again without coming to a full stop.

Too soon, the flight was over. I watched my pilot struggle to unbend from the cockpit, a feat that would have humbled lesser men, but not Bernie.

"I had the landing," he said as he touched ground.

We all congratulated Grandpa and took pictures beside the plane.

"Best flier I ever had," said Tiny, as we headed for the gift shop.

I patted Bernie on the back and put my arm around him. He felt warm and sweaty, and good.

Chapter 19

CARRYING ON

Though mentally strong, eternally patient, and quietly accepting of his fate, Bernie remained ready for a challenge. Wasn't that the way he'd always been? In high spirits he'd gone horseback riding in the Serengeti, rafted on a snake-infested river in Arkansas, and climbed the High Sierras. I had an opportunity to give him another one—a tour of the scenic National Parks of the Golden West. I knew he could handle the schedule.

Planning took energy, and I had plenty for both of us. Once I caught Bernie shaking his head as I whizzed by, brochures and printouts in hand. He looked up and implored the ceiling *sotto voce*, "Why me?"

Fifteen months after the successful biplane ride, we were off. It was September of 2012, eight months after Bernie's ALS diagnosis. I found a tour called Vacations by Rail. Bernie wasn't so sure at first: A train? Why not a plane? But the more he read about it, the more he softened. A Western adventure would be a relaxing way to spend a few weeks away from our house and its impositions!

Deep down, I'm sure he realized it was futile saying no to me, so he grinned that familiar grin.

"Sure, dear," he said. "It sounds great." I was elated.

Starting off from JFK airport, we flew to the famous Palmer House in Chicago, where we spent the first night. As we checked in, we found we could upgrade our room, something we'd never done in all our years together.

"Why not?" Bernie said. After that, I knew the trip would be a keeper.

We walked to the Art Institute of Chicago two blocks away, which was slow going. While we rested on a bench in the lobby, Bernie asked, "Where's the Dot Guy?" I played along, no longer embarrassed by his corny comments.

"You mean Georges Seurat, the artist who painted *Sunday on La Grande Jatte?*"

Bernie smiled and nodded.

"Yeah, that's the one," he said.

We ate at Berghoff's, the famous German restaurant where Bernie took me on my first trip to Chicago in 1959. In spite of the oversized helpings of sauerbraten and dumplings, he said, "No restaurant can match up to my mother's German cooking." Where had I heard *that* before?

When Bernie asked me to take a photo of his piled-high plate, I laughed and happily obliged. German restaurants were scarce on Long Island, and it would be something to show the kids.

The next morning Union Station was as I had imagined it—crowded and confusing. There we found our tour leader, who guided all twenty of us fellow travelers to the proper car that would take us all to Salt Lake City. From there, we'd go by bus through Yellowstone, Colorado, Wyoming, and South Dakota, before ending in Rapid City.

Our tripmates were fun and the beauty surrounding us, inspiring. Someone said of Sundance, Wyoming, "The climate here is so damn good, you have to kill a man to start a cemetery."

Bernie liked being in those wild cowboy towns of yore. We strolled the streets of colorful Deadwood, South Dakota, and ended up in a saloon with four fellow tourists—two London gals and a couple from Devon, England. It wasn't those stops and remarkable sites that mattered to me most, though. It was capturing the moments.

We both agreed it was a trip to remember, especially Yellowstone and the Badlands. Back home, as I filled my scrapbook with Western folklore and photos, Bernie said, "Honey, I liked the trip, and I thank you for putting it together, but I never want to sleep on a train again."

Bernie and I rafting on the Snake River.

I'd thought giving him the bottom bunk would be better for him, but even so, he said he had no room to move. He didn't like getting up to visit the bathroom, which was a hike down the aisle for him but only a few steps for me.

"Okay, no more trains," I said.

The important thing was, he did it. He had seen more of the West in one swoop than others see in a lifetime.

The year 2012 was busy for Bernie. He was asked to give an

account of his rescue in North Vietnam at the local American Legion hall, where he spoke with an immediacy that kept listeners on the edge of their seats. Bernie also recalled the tenacity of one particular pilot who didn't return from the war until seven years later.

"My friend and fellow pilot, Spike Nasmyth, was shot down in Vietnam on September 4, 1966. For three-and-a-half years, his mother and sister, Virginia, heard nothing of him. In 1969 they began a campaign, publicizing their family's story to stir up public support for our POWs."

Bernie went on to tell about how the Nasmyths wrote to senators and congressmen, the president, and North Vietnamese leaders. They and their supporters picketed Washington, DC. They rented large billboards along a main highway in Southern California that read, "HANOI RELEASE JOHN NASMYTH." Not long afterwards, the North Vietnamese listed John as a POW.

"By 1970 three hundred other billboards had gone up with 'FREE POW' messages and many POW bumper stickers were distributed," Bernie explained. "Finally, in February of 1973, the freed prisoners came home and Spike was one of them. Eighteen years later, he published his story, *2355 Days: A POW's Story.*"

Bernie took generous sips of water as he spoke, projecting his voice as best he could. It was the first time he'd talked in front of an audience since his diagnosis. He knew he was different. Most of the audience didn't.

As months sped by and Bernie's health deteriorated daily, my internal voice woke up. I watched Bernie waiting for me to put dinner on the table and wondered how he maintained such remarkable composure, considering that he knew what awaited him. He could hardly hold his fork or cut his meat. His breathing was laborious.

As an air force and airline wife, I'd been used to having days and nights without Bernie. Usually, they were time-gifts. For days at a time, I pursued sewing or painting and didn't worry about cleaning up. Now I thought, *Soon his chair will be empty and I'll have to imagine him here and conjure his voice, even his mannerisms.* Every small gesture I made—tossing a salad or putting chicken and vegetables on his plate—seemed to happen in slow motion and take on importance not proportional to the task at hand. It was if my sweet husband was Alexander the Great, heading out for battle. In a sense Bernie was getting ready to fight the good fight—his last.

We endured with the help of ALS Ride for Life, a wonderful group. This patient-driven volunteer organization—founded in 1997 by Christopher Pendergast, an ALS survivor for more than twenty-five years, and his wife, Christine—is dedicated to finding a cure for amyotrophic lateral sclerosis. It also supports patients, caregivers, and families through its patient services programs, raises public awareness, and provides the community with the latest ALS news, information, and inspiration.

The Ride for Life caregiver meetings turned out to be my lifeline in a sea of uncertainty, but my first one was a disaster. My meltdown that night began as I entered the University of Stony Brook's medical school campus. I had difficulty reading the small directional signs in the dark and ended up parking in the employee garage, which required a pass for the machine barring the entrance. My wits deserted me. Finally, I noticed the machine had a phone button. I pressed it and talked to someone who sounded far away. He told me I was in the employee lot, but I kept on pleading. Magically, the gate opened. I felt like an idiot.

I walked the ramp to the building and entered with high expectations. I was going to meet people in my situation. I would have a support group of people who would understand and advise me.

I wandered down a labyrinth of deserted hallways and found the room I was looking for. The door was locked. Was it the wrong night? The wrong time? The wrong room? I cased the halls nearby and then called Christine's cell phone. She didn't answer. After waiting fifteen more minutes, I left, wondering how I would exit the garage.

Shaken to the core, I walked the ramp back with a friendly employee who, after hearing my story, told me to pull my Honda close to her car. She said I could glide out behind her as she punched through the exit gate. Phew! She was an Angel Present—a name I call those who suddenly drop into my anxious world when I need support.

Five minutes later, on Route 27, as I replayed my dysfunctional performance at Stony Brook, I noticed my gas gauge was on empty. *Bernie would never let that happen.* I pulled into the first gas station I saw. It was closed, as were most stores in that strip mall. It was only 9 p.m.

I locked myself in the car and cried, wondering what was wrong with me. *Why can't I cope?* I called Bernie and woke him up.

"Stay where you are," he said. "I'm bringing gas."

I prayed and waited, thinking of my pilot, the rescuer. I closed my eyes and pictured the time, three years earlier, when he flew to Saint Louis to rescue me from another prickly situation. Since I'd retired from teaching, I'd taken on the role of power of attorney (POA) for my lifelong friend, Anne Smith, who was confined to a nursing home. I traveled to Saint Louis often, usually taking care of her business affairs first and then running errands and reminiscing with her.

While flying into Saint Louis that one time, the top of my left hand puffed up like a miniature balloon. I was more alarmed than in pain. I walked up to Marilyn, the galley attendant, and showed her my hand, which was turning purple. I asked if she thought it could be a spider bite. She gasped.

"I'll have to call the EMTs to meet the plane," she said. "I've never seen anything like it."

A spider bite didn't seem plausible. Her concern and control over the situation allowed me to relax. As we waited for the landing approach, we chatted like old friends, as airline people sometimes do. She was calming me down without letting me know it.

As the plane pulled up to the gate, an ambulance greeted us, its lights blinking. I was the first to deplane. Three serious, equipment-toting emergency men sat me down in the terminal for a few minutes, looked at my hand, and took my blood pressure.

"We're taking you to an emergency room," they said. "Which hospital would you prefer?"

"Barnes-Jewish. It's less than a mile from my motel."

I insisted on walking to the ambulance—the first I'd ever ridden in. I lay down on the stretcher and off we went.

"Your blood pressure is 166," the young attendant said. "Is it always this high?"

"Only when I'm riding on a stretcher in an ambulance."

"Oh," he said. I settled down and called my pilot.

"Hey, honey, guess where I am?"

"Are you at the hotel yet?"

"No," I said. "I'm in an ambulance on my way to Barnes Hospital Emergency Room."

"You're what?!" I told him my story. "Not to worry," he said. "I'll be there."

I spent the night in the emergency room, most of the time waiting to be seen. My hand mystified the doctor. He bandaged it tightly, wrote out a prescription for pain, and made an appointment for me to see a hand specialist before I left town.

On the way to the motel, my cabdriver took me to an all-night pharmacy to pick up my new pills. It was 5 a.m.

"Where are you from?" he asked.

"Long Island, but I grew up here." We were passing Forest Park, one of my favorite spots. "It's always nice to be back."

The cabby pulled up to the Drury Inn and Suites.

"No offense, lady," he said, turning around, "but I'm from New Jersey, and I'm goin' back as soon as I can."

Meantime, Bernie had cancelled my airport rental car and booked another for that evening.

"See you tonight," he said. "Hold tight."

I called Anne, took a pain pill, and slept. When afternoon came, I melted into the recliner, one of the reasons I liked that motel, and ordered a sandwich from room service. Next, I flipped on the remote and turned to Turner Movie Classics. It was Saint Patrick's Day, which I'd forgotten. I sat back the rest of the afternoon and let John Wayne, Maureen O'Hara, and Victor McLaglen entertain me.

Around cocktail time, Bernie walked in with two drinks and a tray of appetizers. Things were looking up.

"Boy, am I glad to see you!" I said. He put the tray down and glanced at my oversized bandage. Then he kissed me.

"Hmm, what's the trouble, Little Bubble?" he asked.

The next three days with Anne went as planned. When we weren't with her, Bernie and I checked out our favorite restaurants each night and even went to church on Sunday before we left. When we entered the church vestibule, the greeter asked us if we'd been to their church before.

"Yes," I said, "we were married here by Dr. McElroy more than forty-five years ago." She seemed delighted and surprised.

"He's passed on," she said, "but I'll introduce you to his daughter after the service."

Before we left, we visited the coffee hour where we met the congregants and were treated like dignitaries. When we walked through the sanctuary to leave, Bernie left me and walked up the few stairs to the altar. He faced the rows of empty pews and then turned and beckoned me to join him.

"What's going on?" I asked. My pilot never said a word but drew me close and kissed me.

"I wanted to do it, just like I did on September 2, 1961," he said with a grin. I was overwhelmed, never suspecting he had this in mind. Bernie's kiss was my anniversary gift. It still is. It arrives each September to remind me just how sentimental an old fighter pilot could be.

The hand surgeon said I had a spontaneous bruise—a ruptured blood vessel that caused blood to escape into my hand. He called it Ecchymosis.

"The atmospheric pressure from high-altitude flying caused the swelling," he explained.

By the time Bernie and I left that Sunday, my hand still felt tender, but it was back to its normal size and the discoloration was fading. I wore a compression glove on the return flight home.

Anne was so happy to see Bernie again. He told her that my mystery wound was just a ploy to get him out there. We laughed.

There I was again, at a gas station at night, waiting to be rescued. Except this time, it was my fault. I sat in my locked car in a murky, deserted parking lot in the town of Patchogue. I thanked God that Bernie was coming. He pulled into the lot and parked in the row in front of me. I watched him push himself out of his car, toting a gas can. *How does he find the strength?*

As I drove my car home in tandem with his, I wondered how I would ever manage without him. He'd been my saving grace for fifty-three years. I thought about the beginning of our journey with ALS. It started with a visit to Dr. Doreen Addrizzo-Harris, a Manhattan pulmonologist. She treated Bernie's breathing problems and sent him to a specialist for tests. After those results came in, she recommended that he see Dr. Dale J. Lange. Thanks to Dr. Addrizzo-Harris, Bernie was on his way to a diagnosis.

Dr. Lange arranged all the preliminary tests my pilot needed. It took him many months to come to a diagnosis. Finally, in February 2012, he uttered the words we didn't want to hear: "The diagnosis of amyotrophic lateral sclerosis is inescapable."

Suddenly, all Bernie had endured made sense. His sickness had a name. We visited the Hospital for Special Surgery's ALS clinic, sponsored by the Greater New York Chapter of the ALS Association. We were gratified to know we'd entered a highly professional support system with an excellent staff of clinicians to accompany us as our journey began.

A volunteer at the clinic's Manhattan Caregivers' Group called me often and even included me on an anonymous, biweekly conference line with other caregivers in the tristate area. Tapping me into that group discussion was the assurance I needed to face the future.

Even with all the wonderful support we received in Manhattan, I wanted to meet and get to know other caregivers, face-to-face. Finally, I met Christine and her Long Island caregivers' group at Stony Brook. They allayed my stress and headed me back to sanity. Those Ride for Life caregivers carried Bernie and me through tough times and made our journey bearable. I also learned that if I'd waited just ten more minutes that night I got stranded, the group would have arrived and unlocked the meeting room.

I was eager to have Bernie join in the yearly Ride for Life on Long Island. ALS patients and their friends and family members either ride their wheelchairs or walk, winding their way through the communities of Long Island, ending up at the Brooklyn Bridge. The walk raises funds for ALS research and awareness among students in the schools they visit along the way. Bernie said he wasn't ready to join the ride just yet. I knew the obstacle was having to use a wheelchair. He hated the thought. I understood.

We both supported ALS Ride for Life's annual Baseball Night at Bethpage Ballpark where we saw the Long Island Ducks play—a new experience for us. Since Yankee first baseman Lou Gehrig died of the disease in 1941, a connection remains between the sport and one if its legends. Our son, Paul, came along. Although the walk from the parking lot to the stands proved taxing for Bernie, he never mentioned it. He didn't have to. We clearly saw the effort he exerted and slowed our pace.

This was my pilot's first time in a group of PALS (persons with ALS) and the first time he met Christopher Pendergast. Several in our section, including Chris, were in wheelchairs. Others, like Bernie, were at an earlier stage. The PALS were recognized at home plate during halftime, putting them in the spotlight—a place that made Bernie uncomfortable. The whole experience was sobering for my pilot.

After dinner, several times a week, I was still trying to capture Bernie's memoirs on my laptop. Our little sessions were becoming a pleasant routine we shared. He'd become introspective, a meditator instead of a doer. One night I suggested we pray together, which we'd never formally done before. I asked that we spend the first few minutes praising God and putting our gratitude into words, which at first seemed like a herculean task for someone who had an incurable disease.

The first thing my pilot said was, "I thank God for my wife."

Our personalities were different but we had united to create a special spirit bigger than the two of us—our marriage. I was grateful for that. I knew he was, too.

Soon there was more to be grateful about. Jimmy told Bernie the VA recognized ALS as a presumptively compensable illness. Bernie immediately registered with the Veterans Benefits Administration offices in Riverhead.

Also, every few months, instead of driving to the Manhattan clinic, Bernie and I went to the Christopher Pendergast ALS Center for Excellence, only forty minutes from us. Ride for Life had been instrumental in establishing the place, the only such center in Suffolk County.

One evening Christine and the clinic staff held an informational meeting for patients and their caregivers about a new procedure that helps a patient breathe for a longer period without a mechanical ventilator. Bernie met fellow ALS patient Gary Hayden, a prominent North Fork chef who'd had a DPS (diaphragm pacing system) successfully implanted. He demonstrated how he managed the implant and seemed enthusiastic about it.

After talking to Gary, Bernie wanted to see if he was eligible for this procedure. His breathing was already laborious and it was evident worse things were in store. As the phrenic nerve to the diaphragm muscle fails, patients lose their ability to breathe without ventilator support. The new device stimulated the muscle. When stimulated, the diaphragm contracted, helping to condition it and improve fatigue during normal exertion.

Bernard was segueing into the second phase of the disease. His muscles would weaken even further and start to stiffen. Most likely, he'd need a feeding tube and a non-invasive ventilator. Further into phase three of ALS, he would need a wheelchair and an invasive ventilator. Eventually, paralysis would occur.

Lisa, Paul, and I supported Bernie's desire to find out if he could get a DPS—a new flight plan that also would include placing a feeding tube in his abdomen. When his doctor gave him the go-ahead, we were glad, hoping the opportunity would improve our Bernie's quality of life. The future after that? We'd face it one step at a time.

We needed hope. The Scottish philosopher Thomas Carlyle once wrote, "Our main business is not to see what lies dimly at a distance, but to do what lies clearly at hand."

The kids and I wondered when Bernie would tell his friends he'd been diagnosed with ALS. On a Sunday morning after church, our pastor approached him as we passed in the hallway.

"How are ya' doing, Bernie?" he asked.

"I have ALS," my pilot answered, without hesitation. The three of us stood there, in silence. I was taken aback and surprised at Bernie's candor. Our family's secret was out. The burden had been lifted. The two men continued their conversation as I slipped out, giving them privacy.

From that day forward, Bernie faced the future with gratitude toward those who supported him with love and prayers. He no longer had to explain himself. They knew who he was—the same Bernie he'd always been and yet different in a way they could now understand.

Chapter 20

BERNIE'S LAST MISSION

The insertion of a diaphragm pacemaker seemed to go well at first, but after a few days, Bernie's breathing became painful. Lisa and I drove him back to the hospital. Even then blood clots were developing in his leg. Those clots would cause an infection in one lung. But we didn't realize any of that. Blood clots! Who knew?

I smiled when I recalled how Bernie made the emergency room doctors laugh. He asked for applause and got it. I knew he was trying on the fighter pilot's facade of nonchalance, an attitude he probably used to mask his anxiety before a combat mission. It was apropos. His hospitalization *was* a combat mission.

Lisa and I stayed in a hotel on Stony Book University property. My son Paul and his family commuted from Remsenburg, less than an hour away. For the duration the ICU wing became our home away from home. During our daily vigil we went from Bernie's room to the lounge whenever his nurse tended to his restlessness and those duties only a professional knows how to do. We felt guilty taking a break. At the same time, though, we realized we needed to renew ourselves for what may come.

When we first arrived at the ICU, the supervising nurse, a middle-aged woman with a welcoming smile, introduced herself as Carol Stanley. She said she was also from Saint Louis.

"My office is over there," she said pointing to her open door, across the hall from Bernie's room. "Let me know if there is anything I can do."

Buoyed by her invitation, I knew her appearance wasn't coincidental. I silently deemed her another AP, or Angel Present.

Bernie was in the ICU for six days, fighting the use of the Bi-PAP machine, which enabled him to breathe without pain. He felt miserable. Blood clots in his lung had caused an infection. Soon after two more were found in his leg. After a few days, his lung collapsed.

A cadre of young doctors hovered around me, Lisa, and Paul as we stood in the hall outside Bernie's room. With sincerity, they explained the operation they wanted to conduct to prevent further clots from endangering Bernie's life.

"Will the stents you recommend prevent all blood clots from traveling to his heart and lungs?" I asked.

"No," they said, "only the big ones."

Furthermore, the operation would require them to insert a trach tube in Bernie's windpipe. That meant I'd need to sign a release that would supersede the health care directive Bernie had completed several years ago: he didn't want any artificial device to keep him alive.

Nurse Carol watched from her open door as my kids and I discussed the doctors' plan. We finally made the decision to let Bernie go naturally and forgo any outside means of support. He was seventy-four years old. The decision broke my heart. I had never planned on making such a decision. The directive looked sensible on paper, but to carry it out was another matter. I knew Bernie and his dad had freed his mother from similar circumstances thirty years earlier. I hoped their Giere strength would see me through.

After the doctors reluctantly left us, Carol took me aside.

"I want you to know I've seen what's been going on out here and I think you made the right decision," she said.

I was surprised and overwhelmed at her compassion. I thanked her, wishing I could gather myself together to talk more coherently. Nurse Carol had given me the affirmation I needed.

A few hours later, Lisa, Paul, Pastor Cary, and I met with the supervising doctors in a private room. They recognized our wishes to let Bernie go peacefully and told us what the next step would be. A floor nurse came into Bernie's room after that and asked if she could pray for us. This kind gesture surprised me and made me feel overwhelmingly grateful. We all joined hands and gathered around Bernie's bed as this nurse prayed aloud. Later I learned that the founding director of Stony Brook University Hospital was a man of faith and that praying for patients of all faiths was not an unusual occurrence.

Five days had passed since we entered the hospital. On July 31st, the sixth day, from 3:30 a.m. until 10:00 p.m., Bernie fought the good fight and died as we stood by him. I snipped a lock of his hair and tucked it into a napkin. It was the only tangible part of him I could take with me. I would add it to the lock of his baby hair that Gretel had saved in 1939. The circle of life was complete. I held Bernie's hand, so soft and pliable, and recited Psalm 23 along with my private goodbyes. Lisa and Paul paid their respects, too. Then we all came together in our sorrow.

Donating Bernie's body for ALS research had occurred to me, but I'd thought my pilot had at least a few good years left and there'd be plenty of time to discuss such possibilities. The pacemaker was supposed to improve things; I'd thought there'd be time.

The decision suddenly became clear. Perhaps this was a way Bernie could help others, his last great gesture. He had helped many others during his lifetime. Why not now? I was certain the kids and I would have his blessing if we gave this precious gift to the Eleanor and Lou Gehrig ALS Center at Columbia University. Brain and spinal cord tissue donations are critical to their twofold mission—understanding how neurons degenerate in ALS and developing novel therapies for it and related neurodegenerative disorders.

After talking it over with Lisa and Paul, I took on this quest with a sense of urgency. If I was to give over his body, it had to be arranged quickly. I didn't even question if the research results would affect those currently suffering with ALS. That didn't matter as long as his body contributed to the search for a cure in the long run. I felt it was a positive gesture we could make in Bernie's name. Most of all, it would mitigate our grief.

In this behemoth of a medical center, there was only one quiet place I could talk on the phone and take notes in the ICU wing—a covered walkway around the corner from Bernie's room. I hunkered down on the floor with my iPhone.

Christine Pendergast was there to help me find the right person to call at Columbia. First, the autopsy had to be done at the hospital morgue. Hours after that, the remains had to be sent to New York City. I was told to find a funeral parlor from my area—the East End of Long Island—to transport the body from Stony Brook University Hospital to the hospital in Manhattan. I did. Even as I felt the minutes ticking away, I signed the autopsy papers that needed attention. There was no room for error.

The ICU desk and the nurses seemed to move in fast-forward. I didn't know how they did it, day after day, with so much life and death going on simultaneously. For a scant hour or so, I was a pivotal player in this drama with a professional and caring supporting cast.

Finally, it was all over. My goal was accomplished. I sat back and thanked God and all those around me. Divine intervention had taken over. I was sure of that.

Months later, I wondered if my frantic energy that night was the same adrenaline rush Bernie felt on ejecting from the F-4 over enemy territory. If so, it was the one combat experience we shared.

Chapter 21

COME FLY WITH ME

Bernard Giere
May 29, 1939 - July 13, 2013

A year after Bernie died, I sold our house and moved to a smaller home in New Jersey. The pleasurable setting would have pleased Bernie. My place is bordered by woods. I can see a picturesque pond from my living room and patio. It's even more pleasing to know I'm near Lisa and her family and only two hours from my son, Paul, and his family, who live on Long Island.

My pilot never knew this house, so I can't imagine him sitting in his favorite chair in its favorite place. Everything is new here, even most of the furniture. I brought my Bernie mementos—a wooden propeller that sits atop my tall bookshelves, framed photos, letters, medals, a set of dog tags, and a collection of squadron patches. I even have the survival knife he wore in the leg pocket of his flight suit; it has a hooked blade that cuts parachute cords free.

I kept Bernie's twenty-pound black leather flight bag, packed with training manuals and other papers. The outside is covered with stickers, including an orange Pan Am Crew tag and a decal that states, "Please Wake Me for Meal Service." There's also a sticker with a lion's face that reads, "See You in Kenya," where Bernie once went horseback riding on a layover. It had been a new experience for him. His comment afterwards was, "Never again."

My pilot comes to me when I see airplanes overhead from a nearby airport. Engine noise doesn't bother me. I'm used to it by now. On my early morning walks, I always see a plane or two in the sky, and I love to see them. I wonder if it's an airliner with a story to tell. *Could it be Delta?* Or if it's a corporate or private plane flying low, I ask myself, *Where is it headed? On a jaunt? On a business trip?* Once, after I waved to a flier, his lights blinked. Had they been blinking all along, or was that just for me? Did I imagine it? Maybe, but I'd rather think not.

Bernie's spirit comes to our family without warning, too. Recently, Lisa's daughter, Liz, had her first child—a darling little girl named Julia. When the baby became fussy on the second day, Liz called the nurse. The gal walked in, looked at Liz and Julia, and asked, "What's the trouble, Little Bubble?" Liz burst into tears. That's what her grandpa used to say to her all the time. She hadn't heard the expression in years.

A few months ago, Lisa and I were busy in her kitchen. The Pandora app provided our background piano music as we prepared dinner. Lisa stood at the sink.

"Dad, give me a sign," she whispered. Suddenly, Frank Sinatra blared from her iPhone speaker, "Come fly with me—" We stopped and stared at each other.

"What happened?" I asked. Lisa looked at her app, then at me.

"I asked Dad to give me a sign," she said. Our eyes watered. "It's Dad. He's come again." Lisa and I tossed up cheers. When Sinatra's song ended, the station switched on its own and resumed playing piano music. What a night!

I always carry the memory of Bernie's love inside me. My children and their children do, too. We invite him to come again anytime, and make us laugh, just like he used to.

Epilogue

Four deer gaze out from the tree line and notice the mourners are gone. They amble among the tombstones, looking for leavings. These graceful creatures are oblivious to my nearness, and I like it that way. Their regal presence gives Calverton National Cemetery on Long Island the solemnity it deserves.

Today I'm adding another chapter to my story, or, should I say, *our* story. I'm visiting Section 29a, a burial space the size of a football field, where Bernie's plot lies. It's 2019, six years after he died. I walk down the center aisle until I reach the tenth row from the tree line. Then head left until I reach Bernie's spot. I'm padded with tissues and have my cell phone camera at the ready.

I run my hand along the top of his stone. It's cool and smooth to the touch. I place my pebble there and stand until I can think of nothing more to tell him this time. Pebbles lie atop several gravestones, a touching gesture from a long-ago Jewish tradition used now by mourners of all faiths. They keep a tangible tally of who was there. This gesture is apt for me and Bernie. My pebble means, *I am still connected to you in love and memory. Rock solid.*

I'm heartened by the gravestone inscriptions near Bernie's: "A precious soul, a true gentleman;" "Courageous dad, a storyteller;" and my favorite; "Our dearest dad who loved us little chickens." The flower arrangements will fade and disappear, but those headstones will last for two hundred years or more.

My eyes drift beyond 29a. I think of the other sections I pass every time I come and how the magnitude of this landscape visits me anew each time. It isn't just the war campaigns that tie these unique souls together in the public's eye. It's the air of *gravitas* that wells up from all the tombstones, in formation, demanding attention and respect.

I find solace in acknowledging my loss. My gratitude takes over when I think of how my pilot's spirit has become my GPS in life. Without a doubt, I am what I am because of him. I thank the Lord for Bernie and our many years together. Dietrich Bonhoeffer must have had me in mind when he wrote, "Gratitude changes the pangs of memory into a tranquil joy."

Widowhood becomes more rational to me as I look around at the growing community of citizens in Section 29a. Its residents have traveled down similar pathways and have their own stories to tell, just like I do.

A small, green tractor chugs closer as it plods along the narrow road that delineates the sections. The groundskeeper is one of many who keep these one thousand acres immaculate. Seeing him reminds me of what one of these fellows told my son and me on our initial visit.

"We treat those buried here as family," he said.

"This is the place for Dad," I remarked to Paul as we drove away. He agreed.

I couldn't help but think of the men who died while prisoners of war, or those still missing in action. They weren't taken care of like family, but they were family, just the same.

Six years seems like six minutes when I'm part of this tableau. I'm brought back to Bernie's burial service again and the plaintive "Echo Taps" being played by two buglers. It chilled me to the bone. I think Bernie would have been impressed. One strain followed the other, but they met again at the end.

It's not easy to leave, but after an hour, it's time to go. I remember myself as a kid and how I hated being dragged to those annual treks to the family plot in my grandparents' hometown. All the grimness and finality of those dead people underfoot gave me the willies. I couldn't escape fast enough. That feeling changed as I grew older.

As a teenager, I was sobered by the inevitable family wakes and funerals. Each one seemed to prepare me for my mother's sudden death when I was twenty-five, pregnant and about to send Bernie off to Vietnam. I learned to endure, with little time for grief but with a heart big enough to house the warm, rich memories of my mother which would sustain me, always.

I recall the services held at Calverton for the men killed in the air national guard helicopter crash. Since that horrific day, I've often wondered what I would have done if Bernie had died on one of his rescues. Would I have been as courageous as the widows whose husbands died that day? What would have happened to me and the kids? If Bernie hadn't returned from Vietnam, how would my life have progressed? I don't know. But I do know that I took the widows' courage as an example of how to go on alone. It's been an inspiration for which I am truly grateful.

In this section, reserved for cremations, the tombstones are closer together, so a spouse's remains can be interred on the stone's opposite side. Although this concept was new to me at first, it now seems fitting that after sharing fifty-four years together, we should share the same marker. I like knowing our testimony in stone will survive many generations.

When I tried to discuss our burial plans, Bernie chuckled.

"Just throw my ashes overboard, out into the Atlantic Ocean," he said.

He couldn't be serious about the subject even to the end, so it was up to me. I'd like to think he would give me some credit for choosing this beautiful national cemetery for him. He'd be glad to know the vets surrounding him in 29a are mostly enlisted men and women. A sergeant once told me, "Colonel Giere was known by the rank-and-file national guardsmen as one of their own."

As for his epitaph, he'd probably scoff at the inscription I chose beneath the tally of medals he'd earned. It reads, "Nerves of Steel, Heart of Gold." But then, Bernie didn't have much to say about that, either. That chapter is mine to write.

The Giere family

"Nothing can make up for the absence of
someone whom we love…
It is nonsense to say that God fills the gap
God doesn't fill it.
But on the contrary, God keeps it empty and
so helps us to keep alive
Our former communication with each other,
even at the cost of pain…
The dearer and richer the memories
the more difficult the separation.
But gratitude changes the pang of memories
into a tranquil joy.
The beauties of the past are borne,
not as a thorn in the flesh,
but as a precious gift in themselves."

— Diedrich Bonhoeffer,
German theologian, pastor, and anti-Nazi dissident,
writing from prison to his fiancé, Maria, 1943.

Acknowledgments

I applaud my book editor, Lorraine Ash, whose enthusiasm convinced me I had an audience for my story. She championed my memoir, gave it a title, and with insightful analysis, guided me along the path to publishing. For your great heart and unconditional support, I thank you, Lorraine.

I thank my friends and family, who lifted me up during difficult times and cheered me on as I was writing this memoir.

Thanks also to those who inspired me to write, beginning with Miss Fox, my sixth-grade teacher, who gave me time and place to collaborate on a western novel with my best friend, Anne Fishbein.

For encouraging me in all my written endeavors, especially this book, I thank Mark Berent. A fighter pilot in the Korean War and in Vietnam, he's the author of four powerful novels about the men who served in Vietnam. He's not only my cousin but a great friend. Mark shared his love of flying with Bernie and shares his love of writing with me.

I thank Danny Bridges, Bernie's Vietnam roommate, and Pete Hoyt, a Vietnam Vet who flew with Bernie in the guard. Both helped me with details I wouldn't otherwise have known. They are true friends.

My gratitude also goes to Marijane Meaker and the Ashawagh Hall Writers of East Hampton who inspired me to publish my writing and told me about Breadloaf, a writers' haven in Vermont. I attended two summers. There I worked with the late Nancy Willard who convinced me of the validity of my story and that it had wings of its own and would be compelling for readers. I thank her.

I thank Joi Nobisso of Gingerbread Books for introducing me

to the joys of writing for children. She gifted me with a dose of her enthusiasm which I've never lost—my gift that keeps on giving. Thanks also to Bill Batcher and his fellow writers from The Scribblers of Riverhead, New York, who cheered me through the completion of *The Melody Lingers On*, a history of my mother's family. Writing it inspired me to explore my own life as a memoir.

In New Jersey I've reaped the rewards of knowing and working with Carl Selinger and the talented members of the Montclair Write Group. They listened to my story, piece by piece, and urged me onward, for which I am deeply grateful. I'm lucky to be a part of this remarkable group of talented individuals, and I thank them all.

I am grateful to the ALS Association Greater New York Chapter, especially Dr. Dale J. Lange and his excellent medical clinic and the staff at the Hospital for Special Surgery in New York City. Bernie and I valued the emotional strength they provided as well as their medical expertise.

I am indebted to the patient-founded advocacy group, ALS Ride For Life, which has created a web of support for ALS patients and their caregivers. The organization helped establish a Long Island-based clinic, the Stony Brook University Neuromuscular Disease and Christopher Pendergast ALS Center of Excellence. Their monthly caregiver support meetings gave me something to hang onto. They kept me going. The ALS Ride for Life awareness and fund-raising events provided Bernie and me opportunities to learn more about ALS and get to know others in our situation. I pray to see the day ALS becomes a curable disease.

I acknowledge all the military wives whose husbands gave their lives in the service of their country, whether it was in Rescue and Recovery, Vietnam, or during more recent conflicts. I salute the bravery and sacrifice of these women.

More than anyone else, I am grateful for Bernie, my cheerleader during our fifty-two years of marriage. In my eyes, he's the best man who ever lived.

Bibliography

Aspen Institute. "What is Agent Orange?" Accessed December 10, 2019. https://www.aspeninstitute.org/programs/agent-orange-in-vietnam-program/what-is-agent-orange.

Beschloss, Michael. *Presidents of War.* New York: Crown Press, 2018.

Chavez, Amy. "Growing Evidence of Agent Orange in Japan." *Huffington Post*, December 6, 2017. https://www.huffpost.com/entry/okinawa-agent-orange_b_1607593.

Flanagan, John F. *Vietnam Above the Treetops.* Westport, CT: Praeger, 1992.

Hayden, Tom. *Reunion: A Memoir.* New York: Random House, 1988.

Henderson, Wendy. "Military Veterans Twice as Likely to Develop ALS." *ALS News Today*, July 6, 2017. https://alsnewstoday.com/2017/07/06/veterans-twice-likely-develop-als.

Hubbell, John G., Andrew Jones, and Kenneth Y. Tomlinson. *P.O.W.: Definitive History of the American Prisoner-Of-War Experience in Vietnam, 1964-1973.* New York: Reader's Digest Press, 1990.

Itkowitz, Colby. "How Jane Fonda's 1972 trip to North Vietnam earned her the nickname 'Hanoi Jane.'" *Washington Post*, September 21, 2018. https://www.washingtonpost.com/news/retropolis/wp/2017/09/18/how-jane-fondas-1972-trip-to-north-vietnam-earned-her-the-nickname-hanoi-jane/

Morris, Errol, dir. *Fog of War*. 2003; Culver City, CA: Sony Pictures, 2004. DVD.

Nasmyth, Spike. *2355 Days: A POW's Story*. New York: Broadway Books, 2001.

Vietnam: The Art of War. "2 August 1964: The Gulf of Tonkin Incident." Accessed December 10, 2019. https://vietnamtheartof-war.com/1964/08/02/2-august-1964-attack-on-the-uss-maddox.

Zich, Arthur. "Lay it right on top of us!" *Life*, July 8, 1966.

About the Author

Sarajane Giere
www.sarajanegiere.com

My writing career began in earnest when I published an essay about my teenage son in a national newspaper. I was surprised to learn there was an editor out there who liked my humorous outlook on parenthood. This propelled me to keep writing and learn more about the craft.

Up until then, art had been my passion. From my hometown of St. Louis, I went to Coe College in Cedar Rapids, Iowa to study painting under the well-known regional artist, Marvin Cone. After I married and became a military wife, and later a mother and teacher, my love of art grew as did my diaries and journals.

Aside from the classic novels I absorbed, I began to read biographies and memoirs, and was enlightened by the revelations I found. I was inspired to learn how others found the power within themselves to overcome the vicissitudes and tragedies of life. I thought of how my parents had survived adversities, and decided to revisit the piles of memorabilia my mother left me. What gems I discovered! I knew I had a family memoir in the making.

In 2012, I published The Melody Lingers On, the story of my Nolan grandparents and my mother, Patty, the youngest of eight sisters. I was excited to write them onto center stage, to show them off to my family and friends, who were delighted with their performance.

My life was a story, too, adventurous and unpredictable, and I wanted to tell it in order to make sense of it all. My Pilot: A Story of War, Love and ALS, is a tribute to my husband, Bernard, who flew the F4 Phantom fighter in Vietnam and later flew for Pan Am, Delta and the Air National Guard. Writing about my life with Bernie was a long and satisfying journey that has mitigated my grief, and tempered it with a large dose of gratitude.

The great artist and teacher at the Art Students' League of NY, Robert Henri (1865-1929) told his students to find out what they really liked, find out what was really important to them. "Then sing your song," he said.

And I'm happy to say that's exactly what I am doing.

****

Sarajane's essays have appeared in The New York Times and the Christian Science Monitor and her devotionals in several books, including, Love is a Verb. A painter of Eastern Long Island landscapes and retired teacher, she now lives in New Jersey and has two children, seven grandchildren and one great-grand daughter.

"Affliction is a good man's shining time."

— Edward Young

A Note from Imzadi Publishing

We hope you enjoyed *My Pilot: A Story of War, Love, and ALS* by Sarajane Giere as much as we enjoyed working as a team with this author to produce this wonderful book.

You, the reader, are the backbone of the publishing industry; without you, our industry simply would not exist and we depend upon you to provide feedback.

Please take a few moments to leave a book rating, and perhaps a few words for a review. Reviews are remarkably difficult to obtain, and we read and appreciate every single one.

Happy reading!

www.imzadipublishing.com

Other Titles from Imzadi Publishing

Faith Lost

I Found my Heart in Prague

Gabriel's Wing

The Hedgerows of June

The Swamps of Jersey

A Game Called Dead

The Weight of Living

The Red Hand

Dragon Bone

The Other Vietnam War

Vietnam Again

The Rain Song

Going to California

Staring Into the Blizzard

Who Shot the Smart Guy at the Blackboard?

Made in the USA
Middletown, DE
25 May 2021